ADVOCACY
FOR SCHOOL
LEADERS

Becoming a Strong Voice
for Education

Sandra Whitaker

Foreword by Governor Roy E. Barnes

Rowman & Littlefield Education
Lanham, Maryland • Toronto • Plymouth, UK
2007

Published in the United States of America
by Rowman & Littlefield Education
A Division of Rowman & Littlefield Publishers, Inc.
A wholly owned subsidiary of The Rowman & Littlefield Publishing Group, Inc.
4501 Forbes Boulevard, Suite 200, Lanham, Maryland 20706
www.rowmaneducation.com

Estover Road
Plymouth PL6 7PY
United Kingdom

British Library Cataloguing in Publication Information Available

Library of Congress Cataloging-in-Publication Data

Whitaker, Sandra, 1967–
  Advocacy for school leaders : becoming a strong voice for education / Sandra Whitaker ; foreword by Roy Barnes.
    p. cm.
  Includes bibliographical references.
  ISBN-13: 978-1-57886-644-1 (hardcover : alk. paper)
  ISBN-13: 978-1-57886-645-8 (pbk. : alk. paper)
  ISBN-10: 1-57886-644-8 (hardcover : alk. paper)
  ISBN-10: 1-57886-645-6 (pbk. : alk. paper)
  1. Education—Political aspects—United States. 2. Education and state—United States. 3. Social advocacy—United States. I. Title.

LC89.W47 2007
379.73—dc22
                                                            2007014077

CONTENTS

FOREWORD

For all of those who have said "we have to do something about education and we have to do it now," Sandra Whitaker has written *the* instruction manual. *Advocacy for School Leaders: Becoming a Strong Voice for Education* is long overdue and welcome in the new discussion of the dynamics of international competition with education and innovation in the new economy. Teachers, parents, and policymakers are hungry for information on how to improve education, and this book gives the resources and tools to satisfy that hunger.

As governor, I was always looking for the advocates Sandra describes in her book. Education policy is only as good as the information furnished to policy makers. Sandra sets forth standards that allow education advocates to lead by example—how to expand knowledge and information to policymakers and businesses and empower parents. I particularly enjoyed the chapter on the pressures and constraints of budgets. We can all be well informed, but how to balance the priorities in state and federal budgets is where great ideas are delivered or remain just another thought. The public and politicians alike want to know why more money is needed, and the answer that it is good because it is for education spending no longer suffices. But with education advocates who are sufficiently steeped in information and ideas for reform, anything is possible.

Another of the vital components of improving education is involving businesses and parents. Sandra tells a vignette about a parent who wants to improve education but is frustrated by the acronyms and language of education. Who but wonks and practitioners would understand NCLB, IDEA, AYP, and all of the other monikers used in education? Here again Sandra points the way by providing resources and a step-by-step process to becoming informed and involved.

Why is all of this important? Don't we elect politicians and hire teachers to worry about this? Why do citizens, businesspeople, and teachers have to become education advocates? The most cogent reason is that expressed by Tom Friedman in his best-selling book *The World Is Flat*. The answer is that we don't have a choice. There are no longer international boundaries. The longest distance in the world is the distance between an index finger and the enter button on a computer. Service calls are answered in India, goods are manufactured and shipped via the Internet from China, and all the while jobs move across political boundaries that mean nothing in today's environment. When I was a child attending public school, I knew the people I would be competing against for a job were in a pretty close proximity to where I grew up. Our children will be competing for jobs with students in Beijing and Bangkok. This worldwide competition is pressuring business, and business is pressuring our schools for better trained and better educated students. The only way our schools can change and compete is to have education advocates at every level of our society who are informed about the issues and who are change agents—education advocates, if you will—leading the charge. This book will show you the way.

Governor Roy E. Barnes
Marietta, Georgia

PREFACE

Like most educators, I spent the first 10 years of my career totally focused on my students and their learning while being relatively naïve about political factors—in my school, in the state capitol, and in the nation's capitol—that affected what happened inside the four walls of my classroom. I believed that if I dedicated myself to students and became the very best teacher I could, everything else would fall into place. And so I sought out mentors, continued my education through workshops and university courses, and honed my practice. Fourteen-hour days found me reworking lessons, reading professional journals, tutoring students, and grading papers anywhere I could. In the end, I accomplished my goal of becoming an educator that students and other professionals respect.

As a National Board certified teacher, I was sought by others to conduct in-service opportunities, serve on committees, mentor new teachers, and more. But I was not an education advocate. In fact, I was fairly content to stay in my classroom, teach, and work with kids. Although I was aware of the politics in my school and school system, if they did not directly affect my classroom, I rarely got involved. And because I was viewed as a competent teacher, those politics rarely affected my classroom directly.

When I became a school administrator, I used the same strategies that had made me a successful teacher: I built relationships, valued people, worked on the real work, and put myself in a position to advocate for teachers and kids. Of course, the learning curve in any new position is steep, and I did not walk into an administrative position as a competent, cutting-edge leader—just like I did not walk into my first classroom as a competent, cutting-edge teacher. But I worked through the learning curve, found mentors whom I trusted, and honed my style. Still, I did not become an education advocate.

It wasn't until I was invited to meet Governor Bill Graves of Kansas that I panicked about being an advocate for education. In retrospect, I needn't have worried. I met the governor for all of a few minutes, with a dozen other National Board certified teachers, but the incident got the cogs and wheels spinning. What would true educational advocacy look like if it wasn't for the competent educator doing a good job each day?

It wasn't until a year later, when I was invited to participate in a dinner conversation with several state legislators, that I got a full dose of this thing called *education advocacy*. In this situation, I actually sat down with legislators, over an extended period, to discuss education issues. At the time, the Individuals With Disabilities Education Act reauthorization was hot, and the state delegates had dozens of questions about special education and regular education. I was floored. Not only did they want to know about my teaching context and how various initiatives and laws affected my classroom and my school, but they also saw me as the expert. And I was. Not one of the legislators sitting in that room had a professional background in education. Thus began my journey as an education advocate.

This text is intended to help you begin your own journey into education advocacy. You needn't wait for an invitation to meet your governor or have dinner with state legislators. Begin now, in your own school and in your own community. I think you will find that you already have the tools and the expertise to make a difference— in your classroom, in your school, in your community, and for the institution of education.

ACKNOWLEDGMENTS

Advocacy for School Leaders has been a process—a process of unpacking and triple-checking what I know and understand about advocacy, a process of writing a first book, a process of representing the wisdom of others in my own voice and in my writing. To those who have helped me on this journey, I am grateful.

The millions of excellent educators who devote their lives to other people's children and their learning. Without you, there would be nothing worth advocating for.

Tom Koerner and Paul Cacciato, at Rowman & Littlefield Education, for taking a chance with a new author and for their editing expertise. Governor Barnes, for writing the foreword and for being a friend of education.

Sara Kajder, who once told me that writing a book is just stringing 10 articles together. I wish it had been that simple! You were the first person to make me really believe I could take on such a challenge.

Mary Kusler at the American Association of School Administrators, who inspired confidence with this topic and started me on the path—and for reading chapters for accuracy and through a different perspective.

Becky Fleischauer at the Bill and Melinda Gates Foundation, who put me in contact with inspiring programs and people who partner to meet students' needs.

Christy Sinatra, Carrie Neeley, Cyndi Wells, June Smith, and Pat Hughes, all of Albemarle County Public Schools, who read drafts and lent endless encouragement. You were my confidence when I couldn't muster any from myself. Thank you.

Carol Clark, for insisting that I take a break once in a while and for making me laugh.

Carol Hawkins, Gary Phillips, Rob Geis, Linda Brem, Leila Christenbury, Beverly Carr, Sujatha Hampton, Kathryn Baylor, Pam Moran, and Bruce Benson—my mentors. Each of you has had a significant role in helping me to become more than I thought possible when we met.

My mother, Ruth Larson, an amazing teacher, who pushes me to excel. My father, Dave Brewick, who took every tear-filled and joy-filled phone call at every hour of the day. My husband, Jeff, who stopped me from hurling my computer through the window when I was frustrated and who made it possible for me to write for hours on end. My children, Josie and Michael, who are the very air I breathe.

✿ ✿ ✿

Information on the Cristo Rey Network was provided through an interview with Jeffrey Thielman, vice president for development and new initiatives, Cristo Rey Network.

Information on the George Lucas Educational Foundation was provided through an interview with Patricia Harder, National Advisory Board member, George Lucas Educational Foundation.

1

THE CONVERSATION BEGINS

It's 5:45 p.m. on a Tuesday, and Bob is just packing up his work to take home. Although most of his colleagues left school right after the students did, at 3:15, Bob taught an after-school professional development class, which he does each Tuesday throughout the school year. Back in his classroom, like other teachers in his building, Bob collects stacks of papers to grade at home, his lesson plan book, and some notes that he wants to review before tomorrow's lesson, because tomorrow is going to be a big day with the state department of education representatives coming to his classroom to videotape model lessons for teachers around the state. There are rumors that the state superintendent might even show up! Bob wants to be prepared.

As he heads out the door, Bob encounters a first-year teacher who is working late. He stops to see if she has any questions, even though he isn't her official mentor, whose room is located upstairs in another hallway. Bob seems to answer most of her immediate questions pertaining to board and school policies, perhaps because he serves on the school strategic planning team or because his room is closer than the mentor's room. Whatever the cause, Bob fields the questions.

At 6:30 p.m., Bob finally gets into his car and heads home. Several more hours of work sit in the passenger seat.

Clearly, Bob is a teacher–leader in his school and even in his school system. This quick vignette shows his dedication to students, his school community, and to the profession. There is little question that Bob represents the best of the best in this school system. The question is this: Is Bob an educational leader or an education advocate—or both? Although there is clear evidence of educational leadership, the vignette gives little evidence of education advocacy.

It's 10:00 p.m. on that same Tuesday, and Beverly, the school principal, is just leaving the basketball game to go home for the evening. She has logged 18,204 steps on her pedometer, talked to dozens of parents at the basketball game, and feels bone tired, like she does most nights when she finally leaves school. Still, she stops by her office to grab tomorrow's schedule and to ensure that her secretary has blocked out time on her calendar to meet with the department of education representatives who will be visiting Bob's classroom. Bob is one of the best teachers in the building, and Beverly wants to show her complete support.

On her desk, Beverly notices a file that she had put to the side earlier in the day. It seems as if there is never enough time to get to everything, and Beverly knows that this student file needs addressing. The child in question is struggling in school, and the teachers have compiled their formative assessments for Beverly to review before an intervention team meeting tomorrow. She grabs the folder, puts it in her briefcase, and heads home.

Beverly is another clear example of a solid educational leader who is dedicated to the students, teachers, and school community. She values relationships with parents and with teachers, and she wants to step up as an instructional leader in her school and, perhaps, her school system. Again, is Beverly an educational leader, an education advocate—or both?

Honestly, these vignettes represent hundreds of thousands of educators across the nation and around the world. We know a whole lot about education and very little about advocating for education, and there is great danger in that.

Too often, I hear teachers comment that they just want to shut their doors and teach. Overworked administrators avoid serving on division- and state-level committees because they can't put another task on their overloaded plates. It is natural to focus on the immediate needs of a single classroom or building and the students sitting in front of teachers on a daily basis. But without participation in what happens outside that classroom or school, educators risk muting their own voices and allowing those without expertise in the field to gain considerable control over education issues.

As educators, we must reclaim our voice in shaping the legislation that affects our classrooms. We must join in grassroots efforts to improve our nation's schools. We must go beyond our comfort zones as leaders in education to become a voice for education.

PROFILE OF AN EDUCATIONAL LEADER

An educational leader shouldn't be a mystery to anyone. However, for our purposes, we must consider educational leaders to be not those with the titles but those who are really leading our schools and our classrooms into the 21st century. In this way, educational leaders

are proactive;

stay current with educational research;

are about kids;

understand the trends in education and how to implement or weather them;

mentor others;

are viewed as experts in the field of education;

make informed decisions using real data;
take risks; and
stay on the cutting edge of their own competency.

In essence, educational leaders invest themselves in education, whether they serve in the classroom or as superintendents. Like Bob and Beverly, they know how to move kids, teachers, and schools—and they do it well.

PROFILE OF AN EDUCATION ADVOCATE

An education advocate, however, moves that knowledge beyond education to influence people and policy about education. The education advocate not only understands that he or she is an expert in the field but also uses that expertise in constructive, powerful ways. Beyond having professional expertise, an education advocate has a personal investment in education and educational processes. For example, most of the parents who advocate in the special education lobby are not educators, but they have learned about education because of their vested interest in their children's learning. In this way, an education advocate

  is proactive, speaking out before issues carry significant consequences for schools and students;
  stays current with education policy and its impact (and potential impact);
  is about kids and their learning;
  understands the necessity of speaking up on behalf of kids and their learning and of promoting the good of the whole;
  motivates others to get involved;
  is viewed as a stakeholder in education;
  makes informed decisions using real data and timely information;

takes risks; and
stays on the cutting edge of one's own competency.

In essence, education advocates don't just invest themselves in education; they are vested. They are the stakeholders with a real, personal buy-in into not only the education process but also those factors that impose themselves on the educational process. Education advocates don't just move kids and teachers; they move people in general, encouraging anyone who also holds an interest to get involved. In short, these people have power, and when they talk about education and educational issues, people listen.

HOW TO USE THIS BOOK

In this book, I work from the premise that as an educational leader, you already have the tools to be an education advocate. If, however, you do not have education coursework or certification in education, you, too, can become an education advocate using the strategies that I present.

Although each chapter is presented thematically, I recommend reading this text sequentially, not skipping chapters. The text doesn't necessarily chronicle my journey to education advocacy, but it does chronicle a typical journey that bridges the gap between educational leader and education advocate, one that starts at home and branches out to the national level.

Consider this, during my first year of teaching, our school was outfitted with four state-of-the-art computer labs, each equipped with 25, get this now, Mac IIe's! (At the time, these desktop computers were state of the art, allowing each student to store information on a floppy disc. Today's average iPod holds more information.) As part of the grant funding for the labs, English-language arts teachers were required to have students working on the computers for 25% of the class time. What's more, to ensure that the time was spent in the lab, teaching assistants designed a schedule that didn't necessarily account for instructional practice but did account for the time requirement. During that year, the majority of assignments that students completed in the lab could have been done in the classroom with pencil and paper. As we teachers became more comfortable with the tool, we began to consider how computer access could move instruction beyond what could happen without it. By our third year of the grant, we were working as a team to develop a schedule that would benefit instruction. By planning together when each class was working on research papers, we blocked out logical chunks of time for that curricular requirement first. From there, we scheduled other 2- to 3-day clusters of time during which students could work on larger projects in the computer labs. This allowed us to also explore various software packages that would introduce or advance forms of writing and publishing. This didn't happen overnight; we had to allow for the journey.

In beginning the journey to education advocacy, you must begin where you are, right now. Then, you must be willing to take the necessary intermittent steps to get to where you want to go. There are no real shortcuts here. That said, read the book straight through, stopping along the way if you wish, to put into practice some or all of the strategies recommended. I encourage you to look to your local community first before moving on to the "big fish" in Washington. You might find in the journey that the big fish are really in your backyard and that overlooking them can be a critical error in your credibility and in your relationships. Plus, discussing issues on a local level prepares you to discuss them on a national level.

The chapters are arranged to present skills and strategies before their application to specific examples. That said, the examples may provide additional context beyond the opening scenarios for understanding the skills and strategies. Depending on your background with issues in education, you may elect to read the application sections twice, that is, first and last, thereby building some background knowledge and seeing the application.

Each chapter also presents a recap of the big ideas and a few action points. Use those sections (a) to remind yourself of the immediate steps that you can take and (b) to jot down ideas on how to take those steps. The additional questions for reflection are intended to prompt thinking about your own context and to record ideas for advocacy efforts within that context.

The last chapter puts you in the role of a mentor, assisting another educational leader on the road to becoming an education advocate. You might be thinking, "Wait! This book isn't that long, and in a hundred pages or so, I doubt I'll be an expert." That's all true. However, when you learn something and become proficient with it, you become compelled as a member of a community of learners to mentor others. One voice can be quite powerful—Gandhi could attest to that. Many voices, however, lighten the load.

So let's begin. I hope you enjoy the journey!

2

KNOW THE ISSUES

Each day at lunch, Sally takes her home-packed sandwich, chips, and drink to the teachers' lounge to eat with the other teachers in her department. She enjoys this time because she and her colleagues catch up on one another's families, events in town, and their favorite television shows. It's a large group, and anyone is welcome, so Sally also enjoys talking with different teachers each day—even though the group has its regulars.

Today the conversation centers on spring break plans. Most of the teachers, Sally learns, will be traveling to various venues near their town. Sally engrosses herself with her colleagues' and her own travel plans, counting the days until she will be relaxing on the beach with her family. She plans to take a stack of books to enjoy while her children build sand castles.

After lunch, Sally checks her mailbox and heads back to her room for her afternoon classes. As she sifts though her mail as she walks, she skims a flyer about upcoming school events, noting that she will put a couple of the baseball games and the school musical on her calendar. She also sees the pamphlet of summer staff development offerings. Perhaps, this year there will be something that

*she will enjoy without overlapping her family vacation and chil-
dren's camps. She decides to put the pamphlet into her bag to take
home so that she can look through it later. The rest of the mail hits
the trash can as Sally enters her classroom. She looks at the clock—
5 minutes to set up before students are released from lunch.*

It's plain to see that Sally feels connected to her school and to her
teaching context. Eating lunch each day with colleagues allows her to
gain an emotional investment in her school and the people with
whom she works. Sally's commitment to supporting the school and
her students by attending school events helps her maintain visibility
with the greater community and to understand her students outside
of her classroom. In short, Sally appears connected and content with
her position in the school. But is Sally aware of the greater issues that
could creep into her teaching context? Or has she barricaded herself
from school politics, believing that she can shut her door and teach?

*After answering a couple of questions after the bell rings for
lunch, Katherine wanders down the hall to the cafeteria. With the
addition of the salad bar, a request from the student council and the
Parent–Teacher Organization a few years back, Katherine enjoys
eating the wallet-friendly and healthy food from the cafeteria.
Moreover, the walk down the hall and into the cafeteria allows
Katherine to connect with students from previous years, chat
briefly with other teachers, and greet the school's administrators,
who are always on lunch duty. Although these conversations cut
into her time to eat and relax, Katherine enjoys catching up on
what is happening in the school and in the community, and she has
learned to pack a couple of quick snacks to eat between classes so
that she can spare the time at lunch.*

*After getting her salad, Katherine heads to a colleague's class-
room where a small group of teachers meet to discuss a variety of
topics—everything from their families to professional journals to
the local school board meeting. While waiting for everyone to ar-
rive, the group chats briefly about family, but as soon as the group
is assembled, it moves on to other topics.*

The hot topic this week resulted from last week's school board meeting, during which the superintendent recommended that, to meet potential budget constraints, the school board should enforce the RIF (reduction in force) policy regarding hiring for the following school year. Additionally, all nontenured teachers would be at risk for transfer or contract nonrenewal, dependent on natural attrition. Although Katherine and her colleagues understand that the RIF policy doesn't affect them directly and that it effectively reduces expenditures, they believe that some of the best teachers in their school are relatively new hires who would be at risk. Specifically, a new science teacher would likely be transferred, and a new choral teacher would be without a job. Moreover, class sizes, particularly in elective courses, would increase, and that would directly affect several teachers in the lunch group.

Katherine and her colleagues discuss the RIF policy, considering the financial and human aspects of it. Although they have the greatest concern for certain colleagues whom they believe are assets to the school, they also express concern for the other potential options to budget reduction. For instance, if the school board had not instituted the RIF policy, what program cuts might have been considered? Would certain elective programs cease to exist?

From experience, Katherine knows that the RIF policy generally works itself out through natural attrition and that although some teachers may be transferred to other schools, very few are at risk for losing their jobs. As a mentor for new teachers, Katherine appreciates the stress that such a policy places on young teachers and how that stress can push talented young teachers out of the profession. She feels torn as the group discusses the issue and the potential courses of action that they have to express their concerns to the superintendent and the school board.

Katherine and her colleagues feel a connection to the school that is different from Sally's. Although Katherine may socialize with these same individuals outside of the work day, she understands that her lunch bunch provides an opportunity to discuss issues of concern and connect to the greater context of teaching and to the education field. She also sees significant advantage to hearing her colleagues' thoughts on various issues, and she believes that these conversations help her to grow as a professional.

Tim wanders around the cafeteria, "monitoring" the students. Because the students understand the rules of conduct, Tim rarely finds the need to address student behavior during this time. Instead, he spends the time interacting with kids and teachers and keeping an eye on the lunch line to ensure that all students have enough time to eat. He actually enjoys this duty because of the positive interactions.

Today, like most days, Tim sees Katherine and says hello. Yesterday, she expressed concern about the RIF policy, a concern that he shares, and he wants to assure her that he will take great care to maintain the faculty positions in the building. He will be meeting with the building leadership team next week, and he asked that the RIF policy be included on the agenda.

Tim also seeks out the drama teacher to discuss the school musical. A parent had expressed concern regarding rumors about the costuming, and Tim wants to give the teacher a heads-up about it. He trusts the drama teacher to make appropriate decisions, and in the grand scheme of his duties as an instructional leader, this issue shouldn't be a major one. Still, Tim knows that if he lets it go, the parents could take their concerns to the press, causing unwelcome attention that doesn't highlight the school's academic successes.

Before the bell rings to dismiss the students, Tim says hello to various student groups, making sure to wish the baseball team a good season. Although he will attend many of the games, he believes that connecting to students' interests keeps him young. He also chats briefly with Madeline about her lead in the school play and warns her not to let her grades drop while she prepares for the role. And as Sara heads out the door, Tim congratulates her on the 98% that she earned on her social studies test, saying that he had asked her teacher to keep him posted on her progress.

Tim gets it. A huge portion of his job lies in knowing the issues and dealing with them. More than that, he understands that how issues are handled determines how others view the school. Tim ensures that he stays current with student, teacher, parental, and community concerns, thus demonstrating his care and willingness to work with stakeholders.

SO, WHAT ARE THE ISSUES?

Knowing the issues, great and small, contributes to an education leader's success. And, truth be told, most leaders don't need to go far to find an issue to address. In fact, when I was a building-level administrator, I knew that if I arrived at work in the morning with "nothing to do," I would have more than a full plate by the start of the school day. In reality, educational leaders always have long-term projects on their plates, and these often get pushed aside for the day-to-day operations of a school, a curricular area, or a school division.

Knowing the issues relates to knowing which issues are really just temporary fires to stamp out and which issues carry longevity and weight. Once upon a time, an educator, particularly in a small town or rural area, could focus on his or her individual community to advocate for education. Even though state and federal dollars contributed to the budget, responding to community needs guaranteed a school's success.

Consider the agrarian calendar that most schools still follow, whether in a farming community or not. Once upon a time, the harvest dictated the school calendar, and if educators ignored that significant community need, no children would have been in school past Memorial Day. Even this year's television season carries a show, *Friday Night Lights*, that demonstrates my argument. In that show, if the football team wins, the community is happy, and if the community is happy, it supports the school. Now, although some educators may feel as though they still live and work in such an area, they are only partially correct. With the mandates under No Child Left Behind (NCLB), the influx of and related regulations for students with limited-English proficiency, and the requirements of the Individuals With Disabilities Education Act (IDEA), no school, no educator remains immune from mandates outside the community.

Although NCLB and IDEA command the national stage and must be accounted for at the end of the day, local issues can sink an educator in mere seconds. As mentioned previously, creating an open culture significantly reduces the risk of surprises and affords leaders the opportunity to shape how issues are resolved. Although advisory committees provide insights, they are composed of people, some of whom don't follow through as expected or who represent their own interests more than their constituents' interests. Getting the pulse of the people through multiple avenues ensures that leaders have the resources and information to become true advocates.

Consider this: Educators and education associations have flooded Congress with letters, position statements, and petitions to allow multiple measures to determine student proficiency. Why, then, would we shortchange ourselves when gathering data to make critical decisions that will affect our schools and our communities? Use the resources available to you.

Get Out There

Growing up, I attended school in a large suburban school system. In fact, there were nearly 4,000 students in the high school that I attended. Despite that, the superintendent knew my name and the names of the majority of my classmates, and we knew him. Despite serving in a larger-than-life job, he was highly visible in the schools, and he interacted with teachers and students regularly. To his credit, he even played the role of the superintendent in our school's performance of *The Night Thoreau Spent in Jail*. Why? Through these interactions, candid as they were, he got the pulse of the people.

Educators have larger-than-life jobs, but we can't miss this critical step to understanding and unpacking the issues. Whether the conversation occurs at the baseball game, in a parent–teacher conference, after a committee meeting, or in the grocery store, having the conversation gives leaders an advantage.

Read

It seems so simple, but taking the time to read often gets shoved to the end of the to-do list. Professional journals, the local newspaper, e-newsletters, research, and professional books all address current issues. Even scanning catalogs for professional publications helps to uncover the trends. Reading across a variety of subjects allows you to gain multiple perspectives on issues that cut across age levels and disciplines. It also helps to uncover the relationships among issues.

For example, concerns with literacy and the trend toward federally funded preK are inextricably connected. Reading the research in literacy leads one to believe that only the irresponsible practitioner would deny a child access to a structured early literacy experience. Relying on that body of research, one might step forward into offering preK without fully understanding all of the issues surrounding such a decision. Reading the research on preK would support the literacy objectives while offering some additional questions about readiness for school, aggression, and social skills. Relying on one body of research may not be enough to unpack the issue at hand.

Span outside your comfort zone and area of expertise. Professionals in the business sector live and die at the public's discretion, and they know how to stay ahead of the issues and troubleshoot hot spots. They rely on demographic research, trend data, market analysis, and more to determine the issues facing business and to make calculated decisions for moving forward. Business leaders must be advocates for their industry and their product, or they risk failure. Reading about successes and failures in the business sector provides leaders a tremendous body of information about unpacking and addressing the issues.

Get Involved With Professional Organizations

Belonging to professional organizations is different from being involved. Belonging requires sending in the dues; being involved requires knowing about the organization and its mission and acting within that organization on behalf of educators in your area of expertise and those in your state or region.

Belonging to professional organizations certainly includes benefits. Most organizations publish at least a newsletter and a periodical, both of which act as ready sources of information related to the organization's mission. More and more, organizations offer daily or weekly e-mail briefs that highlight key legislation, active court cases, and trends in the field. So, belonging matters.

Acting matters more. Although you may think that you don't have time to involve yourself at the state or national level, you can't really afford not to. Although running for an office often jumps to mind, there are a multitude of ways to get involved:

Serve on a committee. Committee work puts you into contact with others in the organization who have similar interests and concerns.

Attend the conference. Conferences have the potential to be networking magic because they provide unprecedented access to researchers, practitioners, and decision makers. Better than just attending the conference, submit a proposal to present a session, which allows you to express your interests and ideas and to receive feedback on them.

Use the resources. In addition to publications, most organizations now offer blogs, webcasts, Podcasts, position statements, and research to keep members informed and connected.

Run for an office. There is no better way to stay updated on the issues and keep in contact with others than to serve on the board of directors. Because the boards of most organizations include department of education representatives, board members get the heads-up when changes are on the horizon.

Attend the School Board Meeting

If you are a superintendent, you are already there. If you are not a superintendent, attend several school board meetings each year and read the minutes for the ones you miss. School board meetings, quite simply, are local politics in action. School boards debate petitions from constituents, hear public comment on a variety of issues, receive presentations from leaders within the school system and the community, and make decisions that guide the superintendent and other leaders in a school system.

Unfortunately, most school board meetings lack attendance, and stakeholders receive information through press releases and news clips rather than from the decision makers themselves. What the press reports, however, gets filtered through its needs as a business, and the sound bites that remain often don't depict the entire story. To really understand the issues on a local level, there is no better forum than the school board.

Invite Others In

The antiquated notion that a leader would schedule several hours for constituents to make petitions in his or her presence shouldn't be so antiquated. Opening your schedule once a month to meet with students, parents, and other community members at their will garners trust and demonstrates your deep interest in connecting to stakeholders. Nothing can replace face-to-face conversation.

Most school systems require teachers to conduct such forums. We call them *back-to-school nights*, *open houses*, *conferences*, and so on, but essentially, they are reserved times that parents and students can elect to meet with teachers or not. It is during these times that teachers have opportunities to meet one-on-one with parents, to have an open conversation about the students whom they serve. From those conversations, teachers often gain beneficial insights that help them to be better teachers for their students.

It was during such a forum about 6 weeks into the school year that I finally met Kathy's mom. She worked a swing shift and rarely attended school events. And because I wasn't concerned about Kathy's academic performance or social interactions, my contacts with her had been minimal yet positive. But when Kathy's mom walked through the door to my classroom at the very end of an open house, I knew something big was on her mind. She shared with me that she had cancer that had become untreatable; that because she worked in the evenings, Kathy was responsible, with one older sister for three younger siblings; and that she didn't know what would happen to her kids when the cancer took its toll. Although I knew Kathy stayed with her siblings in the evening, until that moment, I was unaware of the other baggage that she carried. The information allowed me to better understand Kathy. Although this issue affected only one student in my classes, knowing about it allowed me to adapt my course of action and to do a better job. Why wouldn't everyone want such an opportunity?

HONING YOUR RADAR

Reading the trends in education is much like reading trends in the stock market. You can't really bank on the daily ups and downs; experts rely on long-term trends. Even after September 11, when some individual stocks fell to bargain rates, experts advised consumers to continue to contribute to their 401k's or other portfolios on a scheduled basis; they did not advise rushing out to buy loads of stocks in one area of the market. Why? Because over the long haul, the stock market would trend upward again and that diverse portfolio would be worth more, in the majority of cases, than the individual stock. In those rare situations that an investor had extra to invest in individual stocks—no problem.

So what? Why the banking lesson? The greater trends keep the market—as well as schools—afloat, and they generally correct themselves over time. The more spontaneous the movement, the less reliable it is.

Look back on the whole-language movement as an example. Although some educators believe that this was the worst trend in education, most language experts disagree. In fact, we all use the whole-language approach to learn language. Can you even imagine teaching a child to speak for the first time if you were limited to phonics? Impossible! And without knowing verbal language—if every word on a page were unknown—how would an individual learn to read? In short, before the swings between phonics and whole language, educators relied on both to teach children to read.

When some school divisions took the whole-language approach as something new and magical to the exclusion of phonemic awareness, the dismal results indicated that such instruction wasn't as effective as predicted. And in the last 15 years, educators have returned to a mixed approach, finding the appropriate balance for various groups of children. In short, the market corrected itself.

Some other long-term movements in education include greater inclusion of students with disabilities, an increased number of students with limited-English proficiency, statewide standards and assessments of those standards, school of choice and vouchers, differentiated instruction, year-round schooling, technical programs to bridge students into the workforce, the addition of federally funded preK programs, and dual enrollment and college credit

courses in high school. Education leaders know about these movements. Education advocates evaluate how these movements will
change their schools and community and will work to shape how
that change will play out.

UNPACKING THE ISSUES

Today, many superintendents have advisory committees that include various stakeholders in a school system's day-to-day operations and long-term planning. Likewise, most principals today have
building-level advisory committees. If working properly, such committees do a great deal more than provide a sounding board for the
education leader; they act as the first line of information and insight into the issues. Because these committees include a range of
personal and professional interests, leaders who value the input of
committee members have access to a diverse set of opinions and
can gauge how the general population will respond to various aspects of an issue.

It is through conversation with such stakeholders, through research, and over time that leaders can really unpack an issue. Of
those, conversation is often the most accessible; research is often
the most reliable; and time is the most beneficial. All should be
used as tools to unpack an issue. Even when time constraints press
in, advocates do the research necessary to plan wisely and to shape
the outcome of any course of action.

Knowing the questions to ask distinguishes true leaders from
people who have been placed in front of the group. Knowing the
questions to ask makes the difference in whether information becomes useful or falls along the wayside. For example, if I want to
better understand why Shakespearean plays appear as a mainstay
in high school language arts curriculum, I need to ask about the
quality of the writing and what that teaches children, not when
Shakespeare was born or where. Understanding impact results in

a much deeper knowledge base than does memorizing facts. The same holds true with the issues. Go for understanding impact.

Here are some questions to consider:

Why is this issue an issue? Whether on the local, state, or national stage, issues don't appear from nowhere. Issues are the result of someone's feeling slighted, ignored, underserved, or mistreated. Determining what happened to bring the issue to life helps to make decisions about how to respond.

Who is involved? Issues don't affect all people in the same way. If basketball ceased to exist as a sport, I personally wouldn't care; however, most people feel quite differently. But in response to such a rumor, athletes, coaches, and fans would all take a stance. Connecting with the stakeholders both specific to the issue at hand and in the greater population helps leaders to gain a wider perspective and to see the issue in a more global manner.

What change is a likely result of this issue? Face it, when issues arise, they force change. Playing out possible scenarios not only allows leaders to respond to stakeholders but gives advocates an opportunity to shape the change.

How will the change affect my school and my school's community? Sometimes, the change necessary to resolve or even address an issue feels like a mosquito bite on an elephant. Other times, it delivers a crushing blow. Generally, the effect of change lies somewhere in the middle. Understanding how a change will affect your cultural context influences how you respond and how you guide others.

What are the possible courses of action, including doing nothing? When planning a vacation, most people map out the various possibilities for travel, lodging, food, and entertainment. Advocates map out issues and possible courses of action in the same way, to find the most effective path to take within the time and means available. Not every family takes exactly the same vacation—even if to the same destination. Likewise, not every school will take the same path with various issues.

How does the issue affect students and their learning? Let's face it. This is the bottom line in the education business. Before proceeding, one must look at the issue from this vantage point.

One Example

I am always amazed at what I learn by simply asking a question and listening to what others have to say. In the case of unpacking an issue, leaders should surround themselves with people who think differently. I can ask my husband how I look, but I know that he will say "fine." If I ask a hair stylist, a fashion designer, a business leader, a friend, and a random 4-year-old child, I will gain a better perspective. I may not like the answers, but they will help me to gain insight and subsequently plan a strategy. Let's look at an education-based example.

Year-round schooling, though instituted in many locations over the last two decades, remains a contentious issue for many school calendar committees. The typical conversation on this issue includes the following components:

- Educators raise the desire to move to a year-round schooling system, arguing that the approach provides immediate opportunities to remediate for struggling students, offer exploratory options, provide time for class field trips, exchange learning options, and so on. Some systems relay the cost-effectiveness of such a calendar, allowing full usage of the buildings and reducing the need for capital outlay. Others say that frequent breaks and opportunities for remediation increases student performance. Savvy educators pull in research to support their position.

- Parents raise concerns that their children may be on different schedules if they are in different schools, that they desire to be off during holidays, and that they will not be able to find child care for 3 weeks at a time. (This assumes a typical nine weeks on, three weeks off rotation.) Savvy parents rally together and create alliances before such issues get to the school board, ensuring that nothing will receive a favorable vote unless they approve it.
- Business owners raise concerns about finding summer help during peak tourist seasons and about businesses that rely on the summer break to turn a profit (e.g., camps).
- Sports organizations raise concerns about eligibility rules connected to academic requirements and the flexibility to travel to competitions during summers or typical vacation times.
- Students raise concerns about securing jobs that will provide enough money for college tuition and about participating in competitive activities that could garner scholarships.

In short, what appears as an educationally sound and simple change can become a nightmare if not planned for and handled diplomatically.

REFLECTING WITH QUESTIONS

Why is this issue an issue? Time. As curriculum changes and expands, educators need more and more productive time with students. Or, fiscal resources. As schools spend more dollars on classroom resources, including salaries, they have less to spend on capital outlay. Or some other factor that isn't included here.

Who is involved? At first glance, it may appear that changing the calendar affects only the employees, the students, and the parents. In discussing the issue in an advisory committee, a leader might discover that business leaders and other organizations also have a stake in the decision.

What change is a likely result of this issue? The school calendar might change.

How will the change affect my school and my school's community? In a large urban area, one school's move or one school system's move may not carry an overpowering impact. Some shifting may occur, but the change won't have the overarching effect that it would have in a small town or in an area dependent on farming. In those areas, such a move would require the support of the entire community.

What are the possible courses of action, including doing nothing? In this situation, there are three courses of action: year-round calendar, modified calendar, existing calendar.

How does the issue affect students and their learning? Although we have a body of research that suggests that year-round schooling yields better results, this question cannot be answered out of context. If, for example, a rural school system were to move to a year-round calendar simply because of research, learning may actually decline if children miss school to care for siblings, to carry out family duties, and such.

THE TOP FIVE

I'm not a fortune teller and I can't see the future, but I would wager that the following are now and will continue to be (at least for a while) the top five education issues on the national radar screen.

The No Child Left Behind Act

The No Child Left Behind Act (NCLB) was signed into law in January 2002 as a revamping of the 1965 Elementary and Secondary Education Act. The primary goal of the act is to ensure that all children, regardless of background, achieve at high standards, as determined by the individual state.

Key Points

Schools must eliminate inequity in standardized test scores for all children by 2014.

Each state must define *proficiency* and be held accountable to its definition.

From 2002 to 2014, schools may take steps to 100% proficiency, called *adequate yearly progress*.

Schools failing to make adequate yearly progress will be sanctioned.

If schools are determined to be failing schools, parents will have some choice as to which school their children attend.

All teachers must be highly qualified for the courses they teach.

Why NCLB Continues to Be an Issue After 5 years, NCLB is up for reauthorization in 2007. Although many agree that the act has brought to light what was once invisible, most educators and education organizations believe that the act remains highly flawed and underfunded. Unless fundamental changes are made, NCLB will be the tragic flaw of public education. During the reauthorization period, education organizations will call for the following:

full funding at the authorized level;

access to and support for specialized programs;

multiple measurements to determine proficiency;

flexibility to design and use growth models to determine progress;

flexibility in assessment for English-language learners (ELLs) and students with disabilities;

support for smaller class sizes;

increased teacher salary and salary enhancements for teachers with specialized certifications; and

support for programs that encourage parental involvement.

Moreover, NCLB has effectively become part of everyday language in and outside of the field of education. The subsequent issues of the achievement gap, teacher training, and specialized programs came into the national spotlight through NCLB and will likely remain in the public's attention until key issues of progress toward state standards, access to rigorous coursework, and gaps in achievement are fixed.

The Individuals with Disabilities Education Act

The Individuals With Disabilities Education Act (IDEA), originally passed in 1975 and most recently reauthorized in 2004, guarantees a free and appropriate education to disabled students in the United States. Since the original piece of legislation, the entire notion of public schooling changed.

Key Points
Children with disabilities have access to an appropriate education in the least restrictive environment possible.

Children with disabilities cannot be disciplined in the same manner as children without disabilities if their behavior is a manifestation of their disability.

Children with disabilities are entitled to services related to their disabilities.

Why IDEA Remains an Issue Although legislated over 30 years ago, IDEA remains underfunded, requiring local school systems to carry the burden of meeting not only the specific mandates but also a large portion of the expense. As such, a piece of legislation intended to touch only children with disabilities has affected every classroom. Additionally, appropriate assessment of children with disabilities remains tricky as educators seek to assess academic achievement.

Finally, special education serves a lot of students. According to the National Center for Education Statistics (2006), IDEA served over 6.6 million children in 2003–2004, representing nearly 14% of the nation's student population. And the National Education Association (2006) reports that in the same year, the federal government funded less that 20% of the promised 40% of the national average per pupil expenditure for every child in special education. Moreover, those 6.6 million children have parents who have created a strong, effective special education lobby—both good and visible.

PreK

A developing body of research concludes that the earlier a child receives formal instruction, especially in literacy, the more likely he or she is to be successful. Unfortunately, not everyone in the United States can afford private preschool. In 1995, the U.S. Department of Health and Human Services established the Early Head Start program to serve children from birth to 3 years. In subsequent years, the program was expanded and now serves underprivileged children up to age five. Since 1995, government officials and educators have focused more attention on preK programs and their benefits.

Key Points

The High/Scope Educational Research Foundation Perry Preschool study (Schweinhart, 2005) found that 40-year-olds who had attended a structured preschool program (program group) as children were likely to graduate from high school, earn more money, own their own homes, and have committed fewer crimes than students in the nonprogram group.

Universal preK reaches children of poverty and affords them early structured learning experiences.

Cunningham and Stanovich (2003) stated that the "act of reading itself serves to increase the achievement differences among children" and that early literacy instruction seeks to minimize the "Matthew effect" in reading (p. 34).

Why PreK Remains an Issue As stated earlier, NCLB made what was invisible visible. Gaps in achievement have educators scrambling to ramp up instruction and to meet the individual needs of an increasingly diverse student population. If an early start in school proves more cost-effective than current intervention measures, public preschool will become a major movement in the field. Currently, every major education association has position statements advocating for the federal government to leverage funds supporting public preschool.

Education Models for ELLs

According to the Department of Homeland Security (2006), over 1.1 million people obtained legal permanent resident status (often referred to as a green card) in 2005. Although the majority of those residents live in California, Florida, New York, and Texas, only five states (Montana, North Dakota, South Dakota, West Virginia, and Wyoming) had fewer than 1,000 such residents, which correlates to less than 0.1% of the total population in those states. States with small numbers of ELLs see a significant impact of that growing population as they struggle to create structures to address these students' needs. Although not all of these residents are children and although not all of them are ELLs, the influx of people to the United States affects teaching and learning for all schools. Whether restructuring through sheltered instruction, providing additional ESOL services (English for speakers of other languages), or seeking to meet one or two students' language needs without ESOL personnel, school systems will continue to adapt facets of instruction to meet this rising population's needs.

Key Points
There is no longer one place where ELLs live.

ELLs speak a multitude of languages.

It takes 5–7 years for an ELL to acquire academic vocabulary (Cummins, 1984).

Why Education Models for ELLs Remain an Issue English-only assessment policies limit ELLs' abilities to demonstrate academic proficiency. Students who enter schools at the middle grades and beyond may not have enough time to acquire sufficient academic language to demonstrate their abilities and understanding. Mandates under NCLB require that ELLs participate in assessments, and states continue to struggle with creating appropriate assessments for this student population.

Not all ELLs come to American schools with similar—or even any—formal schooling experiences. Lack of formal testing, limited notions of school and school structures, new social structures, and much more, directly affect a student's ability not only to assimilate into an American school culture but also to demonstrate an understanding of academic content. Moreover, a student who has not achieved literacy in his or her first language will struggle to gain literacy in a new language because he or she has limited knowledge of language structures and the connection of speech to print.

Additionally, ELLs speak a range of languages, including tribal dialects, that make ESOL instruction difficult. In fact, the high school nearest to my home includes speakers of over 70 languages, and that's in a midsized school division. Although some pockets of like-language speakers exist, bilingual education doesn't meet all students' needs. Sheltered instruction, which layers language objectives onto content objectives, meets more students' needs but necessitates more teachers being trained to work with ELLs.

Teacher Shortage

Reports on teacher shortages span the airways and newspapers. Although some believe that baby boomer retirements cause the shortage, experts indicate a multitude of factors that contribute to the issue. According to the National Education Association (2006), the nation will need 2 million new teachers in the next decade.

Key Points

Retirements have increased. Although many attribute this solely to the phenomenon of the baby boomers, other factors—such as early retirement options, limited or no salary increase for years of experience beyond 30 years, and increased demands on educators—contribute to the number of educators leaving the profession before the national retirement age of 62 to receive social security benefits.

Approximately 20% of new teachers leave the profession within 3 years, and some studies show up to 50% leave within 5 years.

On average, teachers still earn less on the dollar as compared to other professionals with similar education and skills.

Why Teacher Shortage Will Remain an Issue   Although states and local school systems work to recruit and retain teachers, we are simply losing more teachers than we are gaining. Salaries, working conditions, lack of support, and stress contribute not only to the decline of people entering the profession but also to retention difficulties. The move to standards, accountability, and assessment changed instruction; school isn't what it used to be. For many professionals, those changes make teaching an unattractive prospect.

The subsequent issues of alternate routes to certification, pay for performance, mentoring, teacher preparation programs, and highly qualified requirements under NCLB will keep this issue in the spotlight.

A BALANCING ACT

No school or school system remains immune from legislation, but focusing on only federal and state requirements will leave your community members feeling left out in the cold. So, although the top five issues remain on the national stage, leaders must learn to balance local issues with federal and state mandates and national trends. There are no easy answers—ever. Finding the most appropriate course of action is a balancing act.

KEY IDEAS

Congressional leaders know that even though "it's all about home," they can't neglect the fact that they play in the national arena. Like our elected representatives, educators must learn to balance local and national issues and to utilize the expertise and services of education organizations to do so.

Using a variety of resources to determine the issues yields more accurate and useful information than does relying on one or two sources.

Asking questions from a variety of perspectives allows one to unpack an issue and plan for appropriate next steps.

EDUCATION ADVOCATE ACTION POINTS

If you don't already have an advisory committee, start one. Ensure that the committee includes representatives from all stakeholder groups.

Get involved with at least one education organization on the state or national level.

Read a book from the business sector and determine how the key ideas can enhance your abilities as a leader and an advocate. Appendix A includes a list of books in the business sector that I have found useful.

If you haven't done so this year, attend a school board meeting.

QUESTIONS FOR REFLECTION

Who am I most like—Sally, Katherine, or Tim—and why?

What is the last professional journal or book I have read? How did it change or affirm my perspective on issues in education?

How do the top five issues already affect my school and school system?

How do I anticipate the top five issues changing my school and school system in the next 5 years?

What information about the top five issues would I most like to share with stakeholder groups and members of Congress? Why?

3

BUILDING NETWORKS

Janet sits at her desk, fuming over the fact that school pictures would, once again, cut into her teaching time. The pictures themselves weren't the issue; the issue was the fact that last year she lost nearly one quarter of her instructional time to school business issues. How was she supposed to cover the curriculum?

Frustrated, she picks up her plan book, where she keeps all memos that affect instruction and instructional time, and begins to tally the time lost already this year. Four days total—and it was only the beginning of October! Didn't anyone listen?

After last year's loss of instructional time, Janet wrote a letter to the building committee about her concerns, and she copied the letter to the principal and to other building administrators. She even raised the issue at a department meeting and learned that the other teachers in her department shared her concerns. Why wasn't anything being done to correct this?

Surely, if parents knew how much instructional time was being lost to business items, they would share her concerns. Although for fear of looking like a whiner, Janet did not go to the Parent–Teacher Organization (PTO) president. Besides, that didn't seem the appropriate avenue for professional issues. Weren't they there to raise money and sponsor dances?

Shaking her head, Janet closes her lesson plan book and returns to grading papers.

Although she apparently cares deeply about important education issues such as instructional time and shares her concerns and ideas with others in her building, Janet doesn't know how to network. She views her only education allies as those in the field, and although she has taken steps to voice her views, she relies on others with like thinking to validate her opinions.

Tom, a parent of two children who attend the local elementary school, looks at the backpack mail in disbelief. Another fundraiser? Two kids times six fund-raisers each year was costing him —and everyone he knew—a fortune! Tom scans the brochure, learning that the school will earn $5 for every $20-item sold. Couldn't he just give the school $20?

Furthermore, Tom, like many parents he knows, won't allow his children to sell items door-to-door. Besides the fact that every house on his block had children in the same school, he didn't want his children to be out in the neighborhood without supervision; with both he and his wife working, promoting the fund-raisers cut into weekend time.

He had often taken brochures to work, and he always purchased one item for each child, but enough was enough. Tom decides that he must act. He goes to his computer and pulls up his address book. How many people did he think would be interested in this issue? Scanning his address book, Tom identifies five parents whom he could call immediately. He also notes that members of his church, bowling league, volunteer group, and book club might hold interest, especially because his kids often called them regarding fundraising activities.

But what could they do? Even if he contacted all of these people, they would need a plan or at least alternatives. After all, the PTO used the money for causes in which Tom believed—purchasing ad-

ditional classroom materials, supporting needy students to attend field trips, providing appreciation lunches for the teachers, and so on.

What Tom knows for certain is that he doesn't have a solution on his own. To recommend changes, he would have to gather information about how much money the fund-raisers brought to the school, exactly how that money was spent, and what current and projected needs the fund-raising money would support. Didn't Bill from his church run a catering business? Could they provide a teacher appreciation lunch once a year—or at least provide the meal at cost? Could one huge fund-raiser that involved more of the community eliminate the need for the smaller ones throughout the year? Were there any community partners, businesses, and individuals who could provide for some of the needs directly— without the school having to purchase goods and services at retail? What were the school board's policies on fund-raisers?

With his mind racing with possibilities, Tom decides to gather information and involve others. He picks up the phone to call the PTO president.

The hardest part of advocacy is the willingness to leverage existing networks and build new networks. Although humans live in community, they often isolate themselves from the help that they need to make a difference. To effectively advocate for change, however, those individuals, with their varied perspectives on an issue, must band together to present a more global and unified voice.

Consider this. One student in your school begins to complain about the quality of the food at lunch. You register the complaint as just that, a complaint. Over time, a group of students lobby together to request that the quality of the food be improved. When still dissatisfied several months later, the group of students begins to petition other students in different groups to join their efforts, recognizing that as a unified voice across the student body, they have a better hope of changing the status quo. You begin to register this as a real concern among the students, instead of an individual complaint.

The larger the body of people that a voice represents, the more likely it will be not only heard but respected. In short, networking matters—a lot.

IDENTIFYING THE CAUSE

As seen in each of the examples, the issue doesn't need to carry enormous magnitude to matter. The quality of school lunches, fund-raising, and when business issues are addressed during the school day all make a difference in perceptions and realities regarding school. But to identify the people most invested in an issue, one must identify the issue first.

In the previous chapter, we looked at some ways to learn about and identify issues, to research them, and to ask the questions to unpack them. In advocating for change, however, one must take identifying the issue through an additional step to identify the cause for which one will be working. The issue may be that students don't like school lunch. The cause, however, might be to increase revenues in the cafeteria, and offering more student-friendly choices—such as pizza and ice cream—provides one means for that to happen. However, providing healthier options to support students in living healthy lifestyles may be the cause, in which case neither pizza nor ice cream will likely appear on the menu with regularity.

To identify the cause, consider these questions:

What is the related issue? What are the component parts of the issue? To better understand an issue, one must unpack it, as seen in the previous chapter.
Who is most affected by the issue? These are the stakeholders, the people most likely to invest their time and energy into

making change happen. Knowing this allows you to make logical decisions when designing a plan and when networking.

What change would those most affected by the issue want to see occur? If everything moved along flawlessly, there wouldn't be an issue. When people raise concerns, they generally want to see change. Sometimes, the answer to this question seems quite obvious: Before the Individuals With Disabilities Education Act, students with special needs didn't interact in regular public school settings—special education advocates wanted students with disabilities to be afforded a public education that would meet their needs. Sometimes, the answer to this question can be a little elusive: Students claim that they don't like school lunch—is it the choices? lack of choices? price? quality of food? all of the above?

What is the time frame for making that change? Working without a time frame generally means that change doesn't happen. That may sound harsh, but it's true. Even with the laundry, a time frame exists: The point at which one runs out of clean clothes to wear—that's the time frame for the laundry to be done. College students aside, most people don't wait that long to wash clothes. In short, don't wait that long to effect change.

How will the change affect other aspects of the issue or create new issues? Understanding the potential fallout before starting ensures that questions can be answered thoughtfully and with real knowledge. Regarding the school lunch example, if students want more choices on any given day, will more staff be needed to prepare the various items? Will more choices—thus, fewer bulk-purchasing discounts—raise prices?

Knowing the answers to these questions allows you to frame your work and be clear on the objective and time frame when you begin to invite others into the work. With this information, instead of focusing on an open-ended issue, you narrow that issue to a cause. The open-ended issue asks people to get involved to address

X. The cause invites people to address X by supporting Y measures to reach Z objective.

Whether working as a team to support larger organizational efforts to effect change in Washington or to address pertinent issues closer to home, identifying the specific issue and the change needed allows one to approach the stakeholders most likely to work for the needed change.

IDENTIFYING MEMBERS

Who Do You Already Know?

Chances are that you already have plenty of contacts to begin your advocacy efforts. The real question is this: Do you have their contact information and notes on their profession and interests in your database, easily accessible at a moment's notice? Maintaining records of those people with whom you interact in both professional and personal circles allows easy contact when issues arise.

When working to address educational issues, recognize that everyone has some interest. Even if the issue doesn't affect an individual directly—through taxes, family, business, community service, or some other affiliation—everyone in a community is ultimately touched by educational concerns. Taxpayers want to ensure that their tax dollars are spent wisely. Parents and children want to know that the quality of the education offered will prepare children to become productive citizens in a global economy. Business leaders want to know that the workforce will be prepared to meet the needs of the future. In short, everyone cares. That's great news because that means that the number of people willing to involve themselves in advocacy efforts increases.

Don't underestimate another individual's interest in promoting an education agenda. Even if an individual doesn't elect to participate on a large agenda item, such as standardized testing, she or he may play a key role in a more local situation.

One Experience   One of the schools in which I taught had no air-conditioning in the majority of the building. Only the main office and those classrooms backing the main office got any relief during the early days of school in August and at the end of school in May. Although the school board had taken measures to install air-conditioning in those portions of a school kept open during the summer months, the community resisted funding the installation of units that would cool the remaining areas of the school buildings.

My classroom opened onto a courtyard and had an entire wall of south-facing windows. On a typical day, I arrived at work around 7:00 a.m. just to open the windows and turn on five fans around my classroom. By noon, the room easily hit temperatures in the low hundreds. Students sweat through classes, struggling to focus on the work at hand.

During an open house one year, evening temperatures remained exceptionally high, and although I had kept the fans on throughout the day, my classroom was still sizzling when parents arrived. During the course of introducing a group of parents to the coursework for the year, someone near the back of the room turned on a particularly loud fan in the corner, prompting another parent to ask if the classroom was always that loud—and hot. Yes, it was. I explained that to ensure the best learning experiences for students, we generally worked in groups, with me circulating to facilitate conversation and the work at hand.

Although satisfied that their students were learning the curriculum, that small group of parents became concerned not so much with the heat but with the noise and how it affected their students' ability to learn. They began to see school from a different perspective and understand the need for schoolwide air-conditioning—not just for comfort but for learning.

Inside the Field

As an education advocate, the first people you should look to for support are your colleagues. These are the people most accessible to you as an educator and most connected to issues in education.

A note of caution: One might believe that because these people are educators, they are natural advocates for education issues. Not true (thus, this book). Knowing what's best for students and learning and acting on that knowledge within an education community differs considerably from knowing what's best for kids and advocating for that inside and outside the field.

Most educators are experts at advocating for individual children. They understand that Susan and Cara have different needs—they learn differently; they like different extracurricular activities; they have different support systems. When interacting with stakeholders in Susan's education, most educators will advocate for those strategies and learning experiences that will help Susan—likewise with Cara.

Most educators, however, are not experts at advocating for education needs. Although they may know the issues, they likely know them from the perspective of an individual classroom or school building, thus making it difficult to understand the issue at a deeper level. Also, the closer that one works with individual children, the less likely that person will work with large budgets, the nuances of federal mandates (excepting special education), the intricacies of staffing and scheduling, and so on. Although we expect legislators to zoom in to see the individual child, educators often need to pan out to appreciate the greater scope of the issue at hand.

That said, once educators understand the issue and the cause—and how it affects children with whom they work—they often become tireless advocates *because* they are educators. Moreover, because of their expertise and ability to provide specific classroom examples, educators lend a great deal to advocacy efforts.

Other Stakeholders

Consider all of the groups—every one of them—in a community that have a vested interest in the quality of education that the schools in the community provide. But like you, other stakeholders move in various circles of people and influence. For this reason, addressing stakeholder groups rather than approaching each person as an individual yields better results.

If, for example, you want to know how many girls in the second grade have their rooms painted pink, you wouldn't poll every student in the school. The fifth-grade boys might be insulted by being asked to complete a survey that doesn't affect them and for which their answers will not be valued. The time spent conducting such a large survey would be wasted because the majority of the responses wouldn't be valid. Likewise, targeting advocacy efforts conserves time and money and allows those involved to be and feel valued through their input and expertise.

In working with outside stakeholder groups, consider the following:

Research how and where those groups congregate. Like various groups inside education, those outside education conduct conferences and hold meetings that might provide points of contact.

Is there an organization to which they belong? All professions have professional organizations. In some cases, membership is required to conduct business in an area. Often, working with the parent organization streamlines efforts and makes communication with individual group members more meaningful.

Determine the group's preferred means of communication. Whether e-mail, letters, presentations, or face-to-face meetings, the preferred methods help one work to build relationships.

Work closely with group members. Determine what they already know and what they need to know to support your efforts.

Target only one or two projects and groups per year. Although taking on the world might seem a good idea at first glace, being more selective and determining an extended timeline to work with all stakeholder groups in the community over multiple years will prove more fruitful. Targeting projects allows advocacy groups to focus their efforts and build quality relationships with those involved.

Make clear how supporting education efforts will ultimately benefit outside stakeholder groups. Good schools improve communities. Good schools produce better workers, promote growth, increase property values, and much more. Identifying and communicating which aspect of a top-quality school system will have the most direct impact on the stakeholder group demonstrates that you understand its needs, making the group more inclined to support your needs.

Even if an issue appears to affect only one group, consider inviting other groups with related interests. Although an issue with school lunch may center on students, health professionals, for example, may be interested in lending insight to the school lunch options and educating students on healthy choices. Not only would their involvement provide another lens through which to view the issue, the education component that professionals can offer helps everyone to better understand the components of the issue and formulate an appropriate plan of action.

The most important point of including outside stakeholder groups is to hear diverse perspectives to strengthen the plan of action. Particularly when communicating with elected officials, including many voices demonstrates broad dedication to the issue at hand. As a result, elected officials will be more likely to take action knowing that your group represents a range of constituents and their viewpoints.

ESTABLISHING MEANS OF COMMUNICATION

Communicating with members of various groups, as well as with those outside the identified groups, supports advocacy efforts and ensures that the appropriate message circulates in the general public. By employing multiple means of communication, advocacy efforts reach a cross-section of the population, allowing people with varied backgrounds and perspectives to get involved.

In today's technological age, one might be temped to rely on electronic means of communication—fast and efficient. In fact, one reasonable objective for commanding response is to remain in someone's inbox. But that philosophy can, and should, extend beyond e-mail.

Consider this. Individuals sift through e-mail in mere seconds, determining whether each message is worth the time to open and read. Although the same holds true for traditional mail, the brain responds to tangible, in-hand items differently than to those held in cyberspace.

Fact Sheets

Fact sheets and brochures organize information about a group or a cause "at a glance." In this way, readers don't have to sift through extraneous information to know the mission at hand and to locate contact information to learn more.

These one-pagers needn't be fancy, but they must be professional in appearance. The cause should be located at the top—allowing the reader to quickly determine the information that he or she should read. Background information and key points should be easy to identify and must be expressed factually and without education jargon, which puts potential supporters at bay, thinking that they don't know enough to help. Visuals should be informative, not decorative.

Distributing fact sheets when meeting with stakeholder groups, holding open houses, and other times when people come together around education allows individuals to take away information. Although some fact sheets may end up in the trash can, others will be "recycled"—sent to other individuals or groups, incorporated into another group's information, or used for media coverage.

Newsletters

Many schools post an electronic copy of the school newsletter on the school website, but they also know that paper newsletters reach a different audience. Although proficient with technology, today's parents may use it primarily for work purposes, relying on schools to send important information through the traditional mail.

Newsletters offer an opportunity to comment on a variety of subjects in one communication. Although most newsletters include a letter from a key administrator, the additional information often relates to upcoming events, group member birthdays, and highlights from previous events. Although these items build interest in the education community, they carry little weight beyond the initial read. Thus, newsletters should include information about key changes in policy and advocacy efforts.

Using the newsletter as a tool to broaden the public's understanding of education issues allows it to learn about the issues and immediately relate them to an individual education community—whether a grade, a school, or a school system. For example, including information about the federal budget proposal alongside successes in a Title I program helps the reader make the connection between proposed level funding or budget cuts and the students who would be directly affected. Inviting community members to write to legislators, having provided the key information and the local story, makes their involvement more likely.

Aside from sending newsletters to an immediate community—say, a school community—newsletters should also be mailed to outside stakeholder groups. Not only does this keep various groups informed, but it also builds relationships, treating these groups as insiders.

Technology

Think fast! We live in a world of instant communication. A world in which information increases exponentially in mere seconds. A world in which research doesn't require a library or antiquated card catalogs. A world in which pictures taken on cell phones less than an hour ago now flood the Internet.

Relying on paper communication alone will only place your group behind the more savvy advocacy groups. Although paper communications reach a specific sector of the population, they are not enough to communicate quickly with a cross-section of constituents who may be interested in and willing to help promote a cause.

Using the technological tools available will help your group to stay in contact effectively and to get your message to a large population, all nearly instantaneously. Bear in mind, however, that the use of technological tools, including informal tools such as e-mail, must be professional in their message and appearance.

E-mail   Our technological age simplifies maintaining contact with people whom we meet over time and through a variety of experiences. With the click of a button, we can mass e-mail everyone in a database or identify a smaller group to receive information. But with such advances in easy communication comes some immunity to e-mail blasts or mass mailings.

Also, with the click of a mouse, an individual can delete just about any communication deemed unimportant. And without an easily identifiable address and subject, e-mail gets quarantined in filters or deleted by the recipient.

Savvy advocates know the following tips for effective e-mail communication with stakeholders:

Distribution lists: If not everyone in the database needs every communication, creating distribution lists saves time and ensures that messages reach the appropriate people.

Subject line: Include a subject line that allows the recipient to quickly identify the topic of the e-mail as important.

Priority: Use the priority symbols only when necessary. If every communication has a red exclamation point, recipients quickly become immune to its power. However, if something requires immediate attention, labeling the contact as such allows the recipient to prioritize and respond quickly.

Attachments: Face it—lengthy e-mails annoy busy people and require Internet access to read. Attachments of documents, even memos, give recipients the option to print and read later or to save to a file on the computer's hard drive.

Action points: Including action points in an e-mail with appropriate attachments or web links tells the recipient what needs to be done, and it makes information accessible. Don't assume that the message itself will cause people to act. Include information on the most effective actions and the necessary time frame for those actions to occur.

Websites   "Just Google it" seems to be the motto of the new century. When most people need information, they rely on the fastest means necessary. Websites provide nearly universal access to key information for any organization.

Unfortunately, too many websites don't include enough information, or they are so cluttered they become impossible to navigate, thus rendering them relatively useless. Like fact sheets, websites must be well organized and easy to use. And like any effective piece of writing, the site design should clearly relate to the concepts of purpose, audience, and author.

Purpose: Defined as "something set up as an object or end to be attained," the purpose keeps the result or goal in mind. Moreover, the purpose of a website ought to relate to some multimedia aspect of communication—otherwise, paper and ink serve just as well. So ask yourself, what can a website do for your group, organization, or cause that other forms of communication cannot do?

Audience: It's interesting that the third definition of *audience* is "a reading, viewing, or listening public." The first definition is "the act or state of hearing." Too often, people think of audience as the entity that will simply receive a message, but more important, audience is an act; it requires participation. When considering audience, think action and interaction. A story is just words on a page until a reader interacts with it and interprets those words.

Author: Defined as "one that originates or creates," the author in this case designs the site—bringing his or her own bias, expertise, experiences, interpretations, and preferences to the creation. Writing a creative brief to clearly articulate the project, its purpose with specific objectives, and the target audience will help the author to attend to the most important aspects of the site.

Websites have the capability to move a message to a greater audience than just about any other communication method. A well-designed, easy-to-navigate site not only provides information but motivates people to step up and to get involved. Whether through e-mail contacts, discussion boards, online voting, or testimonials, a site should offer easy-to-access, easy-to-use methods for users to promote a cause.

Blogs Blogging seems to be all the rage lately. That's easy to understand because these online message boards act more like 3-D journals, allowing bloggers to read and respond to breadth or depth of topics related to an issue. At a glance, bloggers see the range of topics and the most recent posts for those topics, but they can also click on a post to see the range of opinions on a single area of an issue.

For example, a school system may post a blog on redistricting proposals. Within that issue, several areas of concern may arise. Let's say that these areas are creating straight feeder patterns within the district, altering bus schedules to accommodate the redistricting plan, and eliminating overcrowding at some schools. When the owner creates the blog, it should carry the title of *redistricting*. Then, the owner can create a post for each topic. Once published to the web, community members have access to the blog, are able to view the initial posts, have access to others' ideas on the topics at hand, and are able to respond to those posts.

Although published on the web and technically available to anyone, blogs can be listed in a directory or remain unlisted, much like telephone numbers. If unlisted, the group leader may limit access by providing the blog address to only a small group of people. Yet, because that address can be passed along to others, one should never post confidential information in a blog. Public blogs, however, provide unprecedented access for individuals to engage in dialogue about an issue. Because users can log in whenever their schedules allow, rich conversation can occur without individuals meeting face-to-face.

In short, blogs help to create an online community. They are a forum in which people can express their thoughts and view the thoughts of others. Keep in mind, though, that blogs are like in-person public forums; the leader cannot control what others will say. Although blogs can put a message in front of the public, their primary purpose is to generate discussion and feedback.

Podcasts and Vodcasts   What? Podcasts and Vodcasts? Less than a year ago, fewer than 20,000 Podcasts were available for download. Today, millions of people download millions of Podcasts daily in an effort to stay informed or to learn something new while on the run. A little technology finally took off. The former MP3 player used to carry thousands of songs on a portable drive evolved into the iPod, and now it seems that just about everyone—ages 5 to 95—has one (or wants one) and, with it, unparalleled access to media.

So what is a Podcast? A Vodcast? Quite simply, Podcasting took us back to the days of radio shows. These 1-minute to 1-hour sessions are digitally captured speeches or interviews that can be downloaded onto an iPod (or computer) and listened to at the user's convenience. Vodcasts are Podcasts that include a video component.

So what? Because users subscribe to Podcasts (much like magazines), new Podcasts get delivered whenever they become available. When the user connects the iPod to his or her computer, *poof!* New Podcasts get downloaded. So, once an individual has subscribed to a Podcast, the rest becomes relatively mindless in terms of gaining access to new, updated information.

Picture yourself or just about anyone you know listening to an iPod, whether sitting in an airport, jogging down the street, or riding in a car. What's on that iPod? Probably music. Possibly videos. Potentially, your group's message.

Simple and inexpensive to create, Podcasts require a computer, minimal software, and a headset with a microphone. True, some of the top-notch professional Podcasts require a great deal more to create, but the fancy pieces aren't necessary for a quality product that will reach stakeholders. A confident speaker and a well-written script can turn your message into a Podcast in less than an hour.

Keep it simple. Podcasting presents a forum to get key information out to stakeholders to educate them on aspects of an issue. Podcasts are not face-to-face forums or all-day workshops. They are sound bites followed by enough information for the listener to feel informed.

Speak clearly. Headsets with microphones work well, and they pick up everything—especially, nervous breathing and sighing. It may take several attempts to get a clear and clean Podcast.

Use a script. Podcasting shouldn't be an off-the-cuff endeavor. A well-written script ensures that the correct message with accurate information will be delivered to users.

Timing is everything. People listen to Podcasts on the run, so their length should accommodate the manner in which they will be heard. Although some instructional Podcasts may last up to an hour, shorter is better. If your issue includes several aspects that constituents must understand to be effective advocates, consider creating a series of shorter Podcasts rather than one lengthy one. If the average commute in your area is 8 minutes, for example, a Podcast should be around 5 minutes; if the Podcast is 10 minutes, at least 2 minutes of your message will be lost.

Once your group decides to leverage Podcasting as a means of communication, use other communication tools to make stakeholders aware that the series is available for download—on your own website or a hosting website (e.g., podcast.net, apple.com, podcastalley.com). Even if individuals do not have an iPod, they can listen to Podcasts via the Internet; alternately, your group could burn CDs with the Podcast series to distribute to those without Internet access.

Networking requires a great deal more than picking up the phone and making a few contacts. Networking requires understanding the issues, articulating a cause, involving stakeholders to promote that cause, and providing means of communication for group members and the community. Effective advocacy relies on networking, and networking relies on effective communication and clearly articulated goals.

KEY IDEAS

Networking matters.
Diverse perspectives deepen understanding.

Effective communication keeps allies in contact and promotes your group's message.

Use the resources available.

EDUCATION ADVOCATE ACTION POINTS

Build your Outlook contacts—or Rolodex—and touch base with each person or group regularly.

Work to build a positive, mutual, and working relationship with one or two stakeholder groups each year.

Investigate a new means of communicating with stakeholder groups. Employ it and get feedback on its effectiveness for the population you seek to reach.

QUESTIONS FOR REFLECTION

How thick is my Rolodex? What real information about stakeholders is available at my fingertips?

Which issues or causes in my school or school system will be best addressed at the local level?

What evidence do I have that I include all stakeholder groups in discussion of issues?

Which communication tools do I employ effectively? What evidence do I have?

Which communication tools should I explore? Who do I think they will reach?

4

HOME SWEET HOME

*L*ucy is angry. She is angry with her child's teachers. She is angry with the school principal. She is angry with the director of instruction. She is angry with the superintendent. She is angry about the curriculum, instructional practices in her child's classrooms, and the direction that the school system is taking. And she wants somebody to DO something.

Sitting at her computer, Lucy searches various school systems' websites and education organizations' websites trying to find information about sound curriculum and instructional practices. Although baffled by the range and volume of information, she searches, desperate to find some statement, some policy, something that she might use to combat the ills against her child. She doesn't necessarily know what should be done, but she knows that the countless worksheets, 10-word vocabulary and spelling lists, and low-level questions aren't helping her child to learn enough to compete in a global community.

Tempted to call anyone who might listen, Lucy picks up the phone. Staring at the computer screen, she puts the phone down and begins to cry. She is a parent, not a professional educator. She *wants to speak out, but she feels overwhelmed. Weren't the professionals supposed to help her? Weren't they supposed to help her child?*

❖ ❖ ❖

Rusty looks over the paperwork for the choir's participation in the state music festival. He muses about the advantages of living in the host city—the annual invitation to participate, the experience that the festival provides for students, the exposure in the community. Yes, he always submits this paperwork on time, and this year is no exception. With the desire to take the select chorus to a competition in Greece next spring, he needs all the help that he can get to kick off fund-raising efforts.

Looking out at the spring day, Rusty thinks about the newly selected group of students. They have an enormous amount of talent; they can be tough competitors come next spring. Perhaps, they can raise funds performing at various events throughout the year. That would increase their confidence in front of groups while meeting a financial need.

Rusty ponders how he can get the message out—the school website, word of mouth, parents, parents' businesses, the local paper. Perhaps, he can even turn media coverage into an advertisement of sorts. He knew that the local paper would cover the festival, as would the local news stations. Plus, the October festival would not only give the group time to gather its repertoire but still allow exposure before holiday events. A smile crosses Rusty's face as he considers the possibilities.

The first and safest place to engage in education advocacy is in one's own community. Starting at home allows educational leaders to work with and gain input from those closest to their educational context, allowing them to advance those aspects of education most important to a specific community.

Additionally, small efforts within a community will often see results in a reasonably short period. If, for example, stakeholders believe that each school in a local school system should have a reading specialist on staff and if research and education experts concur, reallocation of local funds and full-time equivalents could make that happen through the local school board budget processes. Taking on the reauthorization of No Child Left Behind (NCLB), however, requires millions of hours and years to research issues and draft legislation. At the local level, issues can be addressed within a school year. At the national level, lobbyists think about legislative strategy in 2-year terms.

CREATING A LOCAL AGENDA

In truth, when it comes to a child's education, the only children that most people really advocate for are their own. Parents view everything in relation to their children. Likewise, business owners view everything in relation to their businesses. So, when taking on large-scale change, whether mandated or not, leaders must take care to relate those issues to the local community and to involve community members in the process.

Know Who You Are and Who You're Not

Lucy, from the opening example, feels powerless. Not an educator, she doesn't have the foundational knowledge to change the system, and aside from her own voice, she doesn't have the amount of control necessary to do so. Without considerable research of the issues and without networking with those inside and outside education, Lucy will remain powerless, except where her own child is concerned.

Lucy's main advantage, however, is that she understands who she is and who she is not. It appears that she has taken measures to advocate for her own child, and she has seemingly followed a chain of command in doing so. Still, her frustration with the system persists. She could call media outlets, but as a single parent voicing a concern, she probably won't get them to jump at her story. As frustrating and overwhelming as it may be, Lucy knows that to make any difference, she needs to know more and to involve more people.

Even the rule makers of *Who Wants to Be a Millionaire?* recognize that no one can be or know everything. Contestants have lifelines to ask the audience, eliminate incorrect options, and phone a friend. In short, they have access to others who may know more about a question than they do. But for those lifelines to be effective, the contestants must recognize who they are and what they know—and, conversely, who they aren't and what they don't know.

Clearly articulating your group's position, purpose, and membership helps to define who you are—for yourself and others. Technically, the purpose portion of such a statement is the mission, but a mission statement alone may not be enough to stay on course. The Nike mission statement, for example, reads "To bring inspiration and innovation to every athlete* in the world" (the asterisk relates to a quote from Bill Bowerman, a University of Oregon track and field coach who said, "If you have a body, you are an athlete"). Every employee at Nike can likely recite the mission statement. Still, a mission statement doesn't include other critical information to define your group. To this end, groups should include position statements and membership statements when establishing themselves and when communicating with others.

Although most groups do an excellent job of defining who they are, they do not generally address who they are not. This important step establishes boundaries of interest and limitations in expertise and resources. I am an educator, author, mother, and so on. I am not a millionaire. So, if I were to endeavor to open a private school focused on integrated curriculum and advancement of the arts, I may have the education expertise, but fiscal (and many other) limitations would prevent my taking on such an endeavor independently.

Lifelines exist to help you stay in the game—in *Who Wants to Be a Millionaire?* and in life. Even within an area of interest and expertise, no one individual knows it all. Using a lifeline to answer a question for which you already know the answer is a waste, and only the unwise do it. But it is also unwise to answer a high-stakes question for which you don't know the answer, without checking with experts in the field. In short, lifelines help supplement and minimize weaknesses.

The same holds true in advocacy efforts. Having a clear under-standing of membership, purpose, and position lends credibility and allows a group to determine its strengths and weaknesses as a group and to identify other experts who can aid in the cause.

Get to the Heart of the Issue

Have you ever received a gift so beautifully wrapped that you al-most didn't want to open it? Admiring the paper, ribbons, and other decorations may have been enjoyable and pleasing to the giver, but deep inside, you wanted to discover what the packaging contained, even if it entailed ripping through the outside trap-pings. Remaining on the fringes of an issue only leads to ineffec-tive advocacy efforts. Get to the heart of the issue.

No one supports ineffective education. Unfortunately, that's what many groups battle against—holistically. They shout at the rain that public education underserves students, and sometimes, they cause a stir. Still, their efforts remain largely unsupported be-cause they haven't unpacked the issues that make public educa-tion, in their opinions, ineffective. In essence, they are like Lucy, unsure and lacking expertise.

Compare that with the example of Rusty. With a clear-cut mis-sion (to raise funds), purpose (to provide a unique experience for kids), and group membership (choir members and their families), he can begin to garner support. When the local paper covers the festival and asks about his group and its goals, he will be ready to provide specific answers, allowing others to clearly see how to help.

ESTABLISHING ACHIEVABLE GOALS

Let's face it. Solving the ills of NCLB realistically exceeds a local organization's capabilities. By the same token, taking on all of a local or state issue at one time will likely yield failure. Advocacy groups must establish realistic, achievable goals that can be accomplished in a foreseeable amount of time.

Look at the heart of the issue around which your group is organized. What is your cause? Are you seeking to increase access to preK programs for children in your area? Are you hoping that the school calendar will be adjusted to allow more immediate remediation or extensions for student learning? Do you advocate for a pilot program allowing high school students to tutor younger children under the supervision of a professional educator? Do you want to see healthier school lunch options? Whatever the cause, be sure that it's doable.

Even on the national level, education organizations don't seek to double program funding in a single year. They articulate positions on specific areas of education need, and they seek to have their positions incorporated into bills and amendments. At home, the same should hold true but on a smaller scale.

To determine what is doable and in what time frame, a group must consider the gap between the current reality and the desired change and thus plan accordingly. If the gap equates to jumping a crack in the sidewalk, don't be satisfied with a 3-year plan for change. However, if you are scaling the Grand Canyon, take the time to get the necessary gear in place.

Discussing issues, the current realities, and the desired changes with the people who have the power to make change reality will increase your potential for success. The local Parent–Teacher Organization president, for example, may know that this year's fund-raising money has already been designated for new microscopes; so, planning to improve the early-reader section of the library may become a 2-year project or require other sponsorship. Working with those who will ultimately make the decisions not only provides insight but affords you an opportunity to build a relationship and offer assistance.

Working with those in positions to make change happen also allows people to anticipate and plan for needed changes, allowing them to work on the offense, rather than forcing them to react on the defense. To know what local school officials and state legislators have on their minds, look at the national agenda—the reauthorization of NCLB, the recent reauthorization of the Individuals With Disabilities Education Act, services for English-language learners, and other hot issues. Searching education organization websites and the U.S. Department of Education website will give insight into the current topics of national debate. Determining how your group's issue fits with or works against these larger trends will allow you to proactively frame your argument and shape your goals.

Once you have a clear end goal and time frame in place, backward-map smaller steps to achieving that goal. What budget timelines must you observe? What filing deadlines will affect your timeline? What indicators will let you know that a smaller step has been sufficiently accomplished to allow you to move forward? What measures will you take to ensure that you stay on track and on message? Developing a clear plan of action increases potential for success.

DISSEMINATING YOUR MESSAGE

In the previous chapter, we looked at ways to open lines of communication among group members and between your group and the community. Use those means of communication and appropriate committees to disseminate your message and to recruit others to your cause.

Using Technology

Recent technological advances make reaching the public a relatively simple endeavor. This can help or hurt you, depending on how savvy you are. Although certain precautions should be taken when leveraging technology tools to communicate issues in a community, advocates know that using a variety of tools reaches different people.

A principal who I know creates a weekly Podcast and posts it on the school website for community members to download to an iPod or to listen to on the computer. This Podcast includes similar information to that mailed home once a month in the school newsletter, but using the technology invites a different portion of the school's community in and makes information available in a timely manner. The school website also includes a variety of blogs about various issues facing his school's community. Recently, the blogs included information on the recommended changes to the high school program of studies, which affects every student in the school. The blog invited stakeholders to voice their thoughts and to read the opinions of others. Following the virtual dialogue allowed this principal to effectively communicate the needs of his school when working with other principals and central office staff.

Use the technology available to you. Web sites, blogs, Podcasts, and e-mail can be effective tools for quick communication and dissemination of information.

Forums

As previously mentioned, nothing replaces the quality of face-to-face interactions. Planning a time when stakeholders can come together to learn about an issue and to network will move your cause forward.

Before planning a forum, determine the purpose. Are you trying to educate others on an issue, determine interest for action, or simply provide an opportunity for networking? Having a clear understanding of your purpose will allow you to plan appropriately and prepare materials, whether a full education component or takeaways for participants.

Because forums are often open to the general public, they provide an excellent opportunity for educating others on an issue. To be effective, use other means of communication to put the issue before the public and generate interest in the forum. Let people know what they can expect to learn and from whom they will hear the information, whether it comes from national or local experts. For instance, make it known that a particular policymaker will attend the forum.

Forums also provide networking opportunities. One forum, for example, can lead to multiple, smaller teas during which individual advocates host small-group meetings to educate about or further discuss an issue. Requesting that participants register allows you to gather contact information so that you can follow up later.

Forums also provide an opportunity for several previously established groups to work together on a single issue. Recently, the Girl Scouts in our town held an enormous pajama party. All of the troops in the area, from Daisy Girl Scouts to Studio 2B were invited to participate. Although the primary goals were networking and celebration, the group created an opportunity for participants to feel more connected to scouting in general, thus ensuring longevity of the program. At other points in the year, various troops will work together on service projects or fund-raising efforts, such as the annual cookie sale. Having larger forums includes the benefits of networking, merging areas of expertise, and creating a larger voice around an issue.

Working With the Media

Gone are the days of three networks, a PBS station, and a sometimes-working UHF station. Even VCRs have fallen by the wayside as DVD and TiVo stepped into the limelight, allowing viewers to watch virtually anything and on their own terms. Cable paved the way for 24/7 news, and technological advances have radically changed the format of news broadcasts. Ticker tape keeps viewers current on the stock market and breaking stories simultaneously, all while the anchor delivers yet another story. No television? No problem. Consumers can view many of their favorite shows via computer, and those news stories can be downloaded as Podcasts. Yes, today's media works in nanoseconds and sound bites.

Even more important than the pace of media work today is the way that most stories break—on the Internet. Twenty-five years ago, breaking stories were broadcast on the nightly news and delivered in the morning paper. The media industry had time to craft the story, triple-check accuracy, and move information to the public. But within hours of the terrorist attacks on the World Trade Center, the entire world had access to video footage, photographs, and interviews via the Internet. We heard stories as they emerged and as they developed, and the evening news rarely carried footage that we hadn't viewed multiple times already.

Moreover, the media has more power in today's world than at any other point in history. According to Global Source Education (2007), "the media has become the dominant force shaping our view of reality and our understanding of the way the world works" (para. 2). And like everything else around us, media is constructed reality that includes bias and perspective.

That noted, what is a school system or education advocacy group to do to promote the needs and richness of education? Here are some guidelines.

Seconds matter. Understand that your half-hour interview will be cut to a 30-second story or a quarter-page article that includes nothing more than a sound bite from you.

Do your homework. It's always interesting to learn what has caught a reporter's attention. Often, local media will seek stories that connect to a state or national issue, so knowing what is on the wire will help you to craft your statements. Contacting your education associations also allows you to learn whether the issue that the media would like to address has garnered recent attention in another area of the state or nation.

Stay on message. Given that only sound bites will reach the general public, it is paramount to keep the message clear, concise, and factual. In a recent interview with a local reporter covering our text-adoption protocols and titles up for adoption, I responded, no matter what title she asked about, that the book had been through a rigorous, multilevel review process before being recommended for adoption. Although I felt repetitive, the story in the paper clearly stated my key message about the process rather than highlighting the individual titles on the list.

Stay in control of the interview. The reporter covering text adoption asked about several titles on our list. Some of these questions related directly to national attention being given to the issue of using religious text in public classrooms. Not wanting to put our school system in the national spotlight for something that would automatically get attached to a much larger debate, I refused to take that path. Stating that exposing students to a broad range of literature across time and culture is a curricular goal, I directed her back to the process by which all texts are recommended for adoption and made available for public review.

Nothing is off the record—even when they say "off the record." Think about this in a different context. If someone tells you a secret, even if you keep it, you still know that information and thus construct a reality about that person or situation that would be different if you didn't know the information. At best, "off the record" faux pas skew the story; at worst, they get published to the world.

"No comment" is, in fact, a comment. With your media contact person (or a trusted colleague), practice what you will and won't say before the interview. If you do get caught, say "I don't know" or "Let me get back to you," rather than respond with false information.

Member check. Qualitative researchers understand the importance of member checking, a process by which participants in a study review the data and researcher's conclusions to ensure that the researcher's understanding matches the participant's understanding. During an interview, ask reporters to read back what they wrote or to repeat what they heard you say, and don't hesitate to correct inaccuracies. If the story will be printed, ask to read the article before the publishing deadline, even though this will rarely be an option. One of the reasons that the article previously mentioned was so accurate from our school system's perspective was that I requested an opportunity to read it for accuracy before it went to press. Although not all reporters have the time to grant this request, make it anyway. It shows that you have a vested interest in the accuracy of the information.

Designate a contact person. Don't leave to chance that the media will contact the most appropriate person to speak to a story. How many times have you seen news coverage of home fires with reporters interviewing neighbors instead of the homeowners? A lot. Reporters interview those most readily available. Designating a contact person allows the media to streamline their processes, and it allows school personnel to defer to that contact for information.

Thank the reporter. Honestly, I dread media interviews, and although I generally deliver a good interview, I always practice with our media contact beforehand. Even so, I am admittedly glad when the reporter finally leaves. I often want to mutter "Thank God" instead of "Thank you." Still, this reporter will member check and follow up (or not member check and follow up) based on his or her perception of my interest and be-havior. Being polite never hurts.

Invite coverage. Make frequent media contacts and prepare press releases about the positive events happening in schools. With enough lead for media deadlines, provide the who, what, where, when, and why for the event so that editors and pro-ducers will know what story to expect before staffing cover-age. Even though many of these stories don't make the front page of the paper or receive air time, you never know when the slower news days will hit and the media will be looking for items to cover.

Press Releases Press releases are succinct statements that give highlights of a particular story and thereby compel an editor or a producer to want to know more. Like articles in the newspa-per, press releases should be written in an inverted-pyramid format, presenting the broad connection and most compelling in-formation first and then following with specific details. Analyzing the structure of newspaper articles will help you become familiar with journalism versus academic styles of writing.

Like an information sheet (presented in the previous chapter), press releases should be easy-to-follow briefs. The main idea should be clear, and it should appear in the title. "County's Teachers Excel" isn't nearly as accurate or compelling as "Seven County Teachers Achieve Prestigious National Board Certification." In addition to providing the necessary information for media personnel to make a decision to cover the story, press releases must contain contact in-formation for the person best qualified to address questions and provide boilerplate information about your school system or group.

Media Kits Although a media kit might include recent press releases, the information it contains should be more general and stable than timely stories. These comprehensive kits should be de-signed to disseminate a variety of information about your school system or group, including background information, contacts for key personnel, an annual report, copies of recent newsletters, brochures about various programs, and fact sheets about your cause or causes. Having media kits readily available at functions allows reporters to quickly gain additional information about your organization without having to conduct subsequent interviews. For all involved, media kits save time and provide well-scripted information pages from which accurate quotes may be taken.

Letters to the Editor   If you are struggling to get media coverage for your cause, consider writing about it yourself. Although some publications may be more inclined to publish letters from authorities on an issue, this section of publications also aims to allow a greater voice to be heard. Most of these letters are written in response to a previously published article (which should be cited in the letter) and can be used to inform, persuade, or rebut. Like press releases and fact sheets, letters to the editor should be concise, factual, and compelling.

LOCAL ACTIVITY THAT BREEDS ACTIVISM

No education group organizes more effectively or moves more efficiently than "band parents," which can actually be generalized to all of the arts. New band uniforms? No sweat. A performance at the Rose Bowl? They're on it. A mere rumor that a program in the arts might be cut? They show up in droves at the school board meeting. From fund-raising to public perception to educational practice, band parents know how to create activity that breeds activism.

How? Such groups call people to action around a cause. They understand that the more ideas put on the table, the more likely the group is to find the right idea to move its cause forward. In short, they work together to find the best solution to the situation.

And band parents roll up their sleeves and do something. If a car wash every Saturday in September is on the agenda, they don't assume that someone else will be there to wash cars. They show up—and they do the work necessary to get the job done.

What specific activities breed activism? Consider these:

Networking. Have you ever witnessed a group of students starting a rumor just to see how long it will take to get back to the originator? Have you witnessed their shock at how quickly that happens? Use networks to spread the word of your group's position.

Defining an achievable goal and the timeline for completion. Without measurable targets, people won't know what to do; thus, they won't act.

Communicating a clear message. Several years ago, younger voters were called on to "rock the vote." This movement recognized these younger citizens' lack of participation in elections and sent a clear message on how the target audience could get involved.

Hosting well-publicized forums. Just like parents who put their children's faces on every issue, education advocates must recognize the significance of and create opportunities for face-to-face interaction with stakeholders.

Doing the work. At some point, rolling up your sleeves and doing the job at hand must occur. Education advocates cannot be above stuffing envelopes, creating media kits, or even washing cars, if that's what it takes to move an agenda forward.

Authentic Communication With Stakeholders

As previously noted, communication is the big key to effective advocacy. However, too many groups and individuals approach communication with stakeholders as a one-way street, essentially saying, "We have the solution," before the dialogue begins. Such an approach yields only animosity and lack of commitment.

Consider this. A family of five sits at the dinner table discussing their wishes for the family's summer vacation. Mom and Dad tell their three children that they want the kids' input and ideas before they make a decision. Filled with delight, the kids begin to chatter about Disney World, the beach, and other possibilities related to their likes, dislikes, and ages. Smiling, Mom and Dad allow the kids' ideas to dominate the dinner conversation. Then, as the family transitions from dinner to dessert, Dad whips out a brochure for a mountain lodge where the family already has a reservation.

The response to such a situation can range anywhere from compliance to all-out rebellion, but even if the "suggestion" is the perfect answer, it won't garner complete support. The discussion participants feel duped and wonder, "If they already had a plan, why didn't they just say so?"

Focus Groups   When conducting focus groups, it's important to ensure that all voices are heard. Sometimes, this requires considerable art and tactfulness because small groups can become dominated by a few strong voices. To encourage full participation from all members, consider the following strategies:

> *Meet in a neutral space.* Schools may seem neutral to educators, but to the majority of the population, they are not. Most people finished high school and left K–12 education behind. They didn't pursue careers in education. They don't go to schools unless their children's needs require their participation. And although the majority of the population harbors no ill will, educators must understand that hosting focus groups in schools gives them the home-court advantage. To inform and educate, meet in schools. To gather information from the public, meet in a neutral space.
>
> *Enumerate the issues.* Listing the issues allows participants to clearly identify the issues and to have conversation around them.

Identify the pros and cons. Asking focus group participants to identify the pros and cons of the enumerated issues specifies a manageable task and gives members a sense of common mission. This strategy allows for open dialogue while harnessing some of the emotional bias that participants may carry with them.

Moderate. A skilled moderator is the difference between a productive dialogue and a free-for-all that produces no useful information.

GRASSROOTS TACTICS—CONNECTING TO A LARGER MISSION

Nothing disenfranchises people faster than feelings of isolation and helplessness. Even if they harbor hope, the other feelings will override it the majority of the time. Authentic communication, organic dialogue around issues, is critical in grassroots efforts.

Even when group leaders have a clear mission and sense of direction, they should work with stakeholders to craft a plan that will allow for maximum participation and consensus-seeking dialogue. For this reason, if possible tactics have already been identified, they should be shared as alternatives, not as absolutes or as a prescribed agenda.

Although working to connect to a larger mission, grassroots tactics must be organic, true to the community in which they begin, and manageable in scope. Think about giving a 10-year-old child a dollar bill and mandating that all of it be put in his or her piggy bank. Resistance is sure to follow. Give that same child four quarters, requiring that two be put in the bank and that two be used for another purpose (to save, to buy candy, or for something else that the child might find interesting), and that child is more likely to comply. Or, take that child to a toy store and ask him or her to show you the item that he or she would most like to have—probably, something costing more than a dollar. Then after the child shows you the item, engage in a conversation about how much the item costs and, together, develop a plan for saving the money to purchase it at a later date. Then give the child four quarters. Most likely, the child—having selected the larger mission, understood the steps to achieve it, and assumed ownership in choice of paths—will save at least part of the money.

Grassroots tactics are no different except that they are broader in scope than a strategy to obtain a desired toy. Inquiry and dialogue must occur before planning and action can begin. The public must understand the mission, and the educators must understand the public starting point before effective efforts can begin. If stakeholders are not afforded the opportunity to invest, they will resist or merely comply.

KEY IDEAS

Anticipate needs to use a proactive rather than reactive approach whenever possible.

Establish realistic goals and timelines.

Use the communication tools available to disseminate the message.

Remember that nothing replaces face-to-face communication.

Think and act locally before acting globally.

EDUCATION ADVOCATE ACTION POINTS

Plan a forum to educate about or invite discussion on an issue in your community.

Make a positive contact with local media about an upcoming event in your school or school system.

Prepare and disseminate a fact sheet connecting a local concern to a national issue, and ask constituents to take action.

QUESTIONS FOR REFLECTION

What is one local agenda item that I can clearly articulate? What is my role? Who else have I asked for clarification or expertise?

What strengths do I bring to the table? What weaknesses?

What evidence do I have that I provide multiple opportunities for stakeholders to get involved?

Which critical friends would best assist me in honing my media relations skills?

5

IT'S NOT "JUST BUSINESS"—
IT'S PERSONAL

A senior in his school's leadership program, Ryan reviewed his proposal, plan, and budget. Ryan's main coursework this semester has revolved around an area of interest that addresses a need in his community. When he first selected recycling because of his interest in the environment, he had no idea that the issue would be so complex. He thought that he would put a few recycling bins around the school for plastic and paper and be done with it.

Over the course of the semester, Ryan learned that although plastic is highly recyclable, his school wouldn't generate enough waste for the recycling company in his town to pick it up. Its policy stated that before it would do a free pick-up, 500 pounds of each sorted product had to be accumulated. When Ryan imagined the space required to hold 500 pounds of plastic, he knew that his plan would need some work.

Thinking that the information he had gathered throughout the semester would be interesting to his fellow classmates, Ryan worked with his teacher to schedule an information day on the issue of resource consumption and recycling and other options to address the issue. Through his project, Ryan was afforded opportunities to meet *with key decision makers and researchers at companies in his community. He learned firsthand how issues of resource consumption played out in his community and in other nations around the globe. Not only was he able from this work to set up the key components of the information day, but he also effectively revised his service learning project to create a recycling partnership between the school and a neighboring business, to launch a program together.*

◇ ◇ ◇

Audrey reviewed her notes before stepping into the conference room. Although she was nervous about adding an internship option for seniors at her high school, as the principal, she knew that she must be the instructional leader in the building. And as an instructional leader, she knew that students in her school needed greater access to the business community.

Located in a high-poverty area of a large city, most students in Audrey's school had started life at an academic disadvantage. Most of the parents had not earned a high school diploma, and all of them worked in low-paying blue-collar jobs—with many parents working more than one. Their children did not have access to books in the home, nor did they gain early preliteracy skills. For some, their first introduction to school was a Head Start program, but for many, their first day in a school was the first day of kindergarten.

Although the school system worked hard to cover lost ground, no current academic program made up for the lack of role models and sense of hopelessness. Now, Audrey had the opportunity to begin to change that. After working with teachers in her school and central office staff, Audrey had the green light to pursue corporate internships. Initially, she thought that the search for an interested company would be long, but she had been surprised to learn that many businesses in the city were interested in creating a partnership. For students who never pictured themselves in an office, this might be the opportunity to open doors to a once-unimaginable future.

Audrey understands that not all students reach their fullest potential in traditional academic settings. For the students in her high-poverty school, having access to models in the corporate world may be the key for students to understand that their learning has purpose beyond the schoolhouse gate.

PARTNERING WITH BUSINESSES

Partnering with the business community is an essential component of education advocacy. Think about it. The majority of the community is "out there," beyond the schoolhouse gate. Educators must begin to investigate new ways in which to build relationships with the business community that move an education agenda forward while meeting businesses' needs.

Too often, partnerships become superficial relationships in which the business provides some product for which they receive free promotion. Those little fast-food coupons used for teacher appreciation or school contest prizes, for example, are mini-flyers for the company, and in return, the school doesn't have to spend taxpayer dollars for these gifts or prizes. Although these more superficial relationships meet a need, they don't move an education agenda.

Instead, many school systems and businesses now form relationships that involve education components for staff and students, learning about an industry and its needs. They create service learning opportunities to involve students and staff in authentic projects that meet a community need. In short, schools and businesses become partners.

What is a partner? A partner is someone who has a stake in your success. Businesses definitely have a stake in the success of local schools and education as a whole. Without high-quality education, employees aren't prepared to meet the changing needs and demands of the business world. Over the last decade, with the surge of technology and the move toward a truly global economy, the relationship between education and business has necessarily changed.

The Demands of a Global Economy

Although technology has significantly changed the face of education over the last decade or so, it hasn't necessarily changed instruction in all classrooms. In their article "How to Bring Out Schools of the 20th Century," Wallis and Steptoe (2006) make the case that trends in education—and, consequently, instruction in the classroom—have not kept pace with the demands of a global economy. Students remain sitting in rows receiving traditional instruction rather than being active participants learning how to think abstractly and in complex ways about information. Wallis and Steptoe contend that a continued focus on minimal reading and math achievement steers conversation away from the real issues that will determine "whether an entire generation of kids will fail to make the grade in the global economy because they can't think their way through abstract problems, work in teams, distinguish good information from bad or speak a language other than English" (para. 3).

However, in the last decade, businesses have risen to the challenge of communicating, working, and achieving in a rapidly changing world. Savvy consumers, more choice in product and services, and greater competition have forced the business community to rethink strategies and to train employees to work and think in increasingly creative and abstract ways. Right now, businesses seek to hire graduates who are team players, fast learners, and strategic thinkers who are creative, innovative, and worldly. To ensure that students will have the skills necessary to succeed in the 21st century, businesses are more poised than ever to partner with the education community.

A Personal Relationship

Although some businesses connect to education as an industry, most connect with specific schools, groups, or individuals. Tommy's Automotive, for example, probably sponsors an employee's child's soccer team, not just any team. Business leaders tend to speak at their own children's career day events. And those donation dollars often target groups or needs to which the benefactor feels a personal connection.

For this reason, partnering with the business community must become a personal endeavor, and these partnerships must be reciprocal relationships, not just funding sources or material suppliers. Becoming an education advocate in the business community allows educational leaders to explore new perspectives on educational issues and to involve business leaders as education advocates.

JUNIOR ACHIEVEMENT

The notion of school–business partnerships isn't new. In fact, in 1916, at the Eastern States Agricultural and Industrial Exposition, business leaders articulated a goal "to work on the general advancement of activities for boys and girls" (Junior Achievement, 2007, para. 1). In 1920, the committee charged with this work changed its name to Junior Achievement. Today, Junior Achievement programs reach approximately 7.5 million students worldwide each year.

Working with corporations in the United States and 100 countries around the globe, Junior Achievement asks corporate sponsors to volunteer their time to teach children about the world and about the world of business. Elementary school children learn about the world and how their actions as individuals, workers, and consumers affect the world. Middle school children learn about the skills of work and the roots of entrepreneurship, including financial literacy.

As one of the longest-standing school–business partnerships in the United States, Junior Achievement has a vision of what business can offer to children. In return, children enter the world of work with business experiences and skills needed for success.

THE BILL AND MELINDA GATES FOUNDATION

Most people know of the Bill and Melinda Gates Foundation for its role in Pacific Northwestern and international communities. And although most assume that a technological component would be at the heart of their outreach, that isn't necessarily true. The foundation takes on issues such as global development and global health and, closer to home, those related to poverty.

To that end, the Bill and Melinda Gates Foundation offers numerous grants and support for education programs that elevate the learning of children of poverty. This section highlights several of the organizations and programs that the foundation helps fund.

Thrive by Five

A new partnership, Thrive by Five will respond to needs in early childhood education and will be built on the infrastructure of the Early Care and Education Coalition. This public–private partnership works with all sectors to gain the maximum benefits of each sector in public and private industry. "The public sector offers experience, considerable public resources and infrastructure, and political legitimacy. Private organizations, such as foundations and businesses, bring expertise, credibility, nimbleness, rigor, and flexible funding to an issue" (Washington Early Learning Fund, 2007, para. 6).

Unlike preschool initiatives to address the same early childhood learning concerns, Thrive by Five seeks to provide readiness skills and early literacy and numeracy skills regardless of where the child spends the years before kindergarten. In this way, children who remain at home, attend preschool, or attend day care will all be afforded the learning experiences they need to thrive.

WestEd and Rethinking High School

"In 2002, New York City initiated an ambitious campaign to transform its public high schools, which, on average, had been graduating only half their students" (WestEd, 2007, para. 1). WestEd, a nonprofit organization, replaced large high schools in some of New York's most underserved communities with 14 smaller schools. According to data from the study, students in these smaller schools have high attendance, ninth-grade promotion rates, and graduation rates—all of which are improvements in areas consistent with national concerns.

WestEd operates 13 major programs that range from prevention and intervention to teacher professional development. Each program operates with one goal in mind: "serving underserved populations" (para. 3).

The Cristo Rey Network

Modeled after Cristo Rey Jesuit High School in Chicago, a school with an exceptional corporate internship program, the Cristo Rey Network is a national association of private high schools that combine rigorous coursework and internships with Fortune 500 companies for students from high-poverty areas. According to the Bill and Melinda Gates Foundation (2007), "part-time internships with local businesses help cover a significant portion of students' tuition and provides them with hands-on experience, marketable skills, mentoring and career guidance, contacts for the future, and a business-oriented work ethic" (para. 2). For these students (the majority of whom belong to minority population groups whose families' median income is less than $33,051), the network offers access to role models and greater options for the future.

Students in the Cristo Rey Network high schools attend school 4 days each week and work at their job sites 1 day each week. The partnering corporations' willingness to work with a four-student rotation in a single job provides continuity for the company while expanding opportunities for the students. Instead of earning a salary, students earn the majority of their tuition for school.

Currently, there are 12 Cristo Rey schools around the nation, and 6 more are slated to open in 2007. Jeffrey Thielman, vice president for development and new initiatives of the Cristo Rey Network, credits this amazing program expansion to previous successes with the work program, which has opened doors to working with new companies. And although the network partners with multiple employers in multiple cities, according to Thielman, "each job depends on a local relationship."

An Interview With Jeffrey Thielman

SW: In your opinion, what is the most powerful aspect of the Cristo Rey Network?

JT: We've found a way to provide private college-prep education to center-city young people. A college-prep education, particularly, a Catholic one, has traditionally been out of reach for low-income families. Our model breaks that paradigm. The Catholic school aspect of the Cristo Rey Network affords educators in the schools to address issues through a lens different from public education. Conversations about values and faith issues, coupled with rigorous college-preparatory curriculum and work experiences, lead to students' gaining self-respect and self-confidence.

SW: What have you learned from working with Fortune 500 companies that other educators should know when starting a school—business partnership?

JT: Building relationships with corporate partners requires educators to step out of their comfort zone in schools and to see clearly students' experiences in the corporate world. Because educators chose not to be in the corporate world, they tend to be skeptical of it, and it's important for them to understand the needs of business for the partnerships to work to their full advantage for students.

The most important thing is to remember that [the corporations] are your customer. Your job is to meet their needs. We learned early on that our kids had to be proficient at Microsoft Office. So, in our second or third year at the school in Chicago, we added a course for all freshmen on computer skills. Although most offices use Microsoft Office, learning the application is only one portion of the computer skills course. Students must know how to navigate technology tools, be comfortable with technology tools, and use skills to adapt to job-specific software.

Students also receive a corporate evaluation as part of their work experience. We tell corporate employers to treat our students just like they would any other employee. And we tell our kids that they have to meet the expectations of their bosses, which they do.

SW: What goals do the schools and companies in the network share?

JT: The Cristo Rey schools want to provide first-class college-prep education to urban minority students. Corporations want diversity. Ninety-two percent of the students in Cristo Rey schools belong to minority groups. Additionally, our program allows employers the chance to form relationships with students who will one day be employees, suppliers, and customers. And the work program keeps students engaged in their education because they can see the purpose and application for what they are learning at school. Students learn quickly how to navigate the different worlds of school and work.

SW: What goals are different? How do you address these differing needs?

JT: I don't think we have different goals. We want companies to be profitable, and we want our students to contribute to the profitability of each firm. If we're not filling a need at a particular firm, then we shouldn't be there.

SW: What has been the most difficult aspect of partnering with Fortune 500 companies?

JT: The work program really brings different cultures together in a corporate setting. Getting in the door and then selling the program can be difficult. We have to help our corporate partners envision students as young as 14 in corporate positions, meeting the corporation's needs. That said, success breeds success. Our reputation and previous successes not only have the majority of partners renewing each year but make it easier to form new partnerships.

SW: How do you continue to keep the Cristo Rey Network fresh, continuing to meet students' and businesses' needs for the 21st century?

JT: We are always learning. We're talking about what our kids will need to know to be ready for work, college, and citizenship. To be successful, kids must stay in school. The more education they have, the more likely they are to pull themselves out of poverty. We think the Catholic component of our schools prepares students for life. It gives them core values they will carry with them forever. The work component gives them a chance to see what the real world is like. Going to work in an office, working with professionals, seeing how quickly things change in the workplace gives our kids a firsthand look at the reality of the 21st century. In the academic area, we're always learning, always trying to figure out how to serve kids better.

SW: What is the most joy-filled aspect of working with Fortune 500 companies?

JT: It's wonderful to see how satisfied the companies are with the program and how the program changes perceptions about city kids. Although one-on-one mentoring is not an expectation of the work program, some supervisors take on natural mentor roles. It's amazing to see the number of supervisors who take off work to attend graduation because they have built up relationships with our students over 4 years.

SW: What else would you like to share about the Cristo Rey Network and your experience partnering with businesses to advance student learning?

JT: We think the work-study program is a win-win for employers and students. The highest rate of turnover in business today is in the entry-level clerical positions. We train our kids to fill these critical jobs. Evidence of the success of the program is a 90% corporate sponsor renewal rate nationwide each year. At work, students are not asked whether they are going to college but where they plan to pursue their postsecondary studies. A result of this interaction with the corporate community is that 95% of the Cristo Rey Network's class of 2005 went to college, and 100% of the students from the graduating classes of 2006 were admitted to a 2- or 4-year college. The program is working, and the demand for new schools is intensifying.

Lessons From the Cristo Rey Network   Building relationships with corporate partners requires educators to investigate a world that they, for the most part, elected not to enter. To do this, educators must be willing to visit workplaces, listen to the needs of businesses, and envision their students engaging in this context. That understanding allows educators to adapt curriculum and tailor instruction to meet academic goals and to prepare students for their future.

To build work-study partnerships with the business community, schools must be willing to take on additional curricular goals to prepare students to work in the corporate setting. Courses to address technology skills, work ethics, and the changing world of work allow students to enter the workplace prepared to meet employers' needs.

Establishing strong partnerships requires selling your program, presenting the win-win outcome that will benefit business and students. Doing this may also require that you address stereotypical perceptions of teenagers or groups of teenagers, such as "city kids," asking corporate partners to temporarily suspend their fears and take a risk. Ensuring that your program will meet a critical need for the corporation, such as filling entry-level positions, helps to create that win-win situation.

Setting clear expectations for the program, including the academic components, allows everyone to participate fully. When asked about the number one reason that students come to Cristo

Rey schools, knowing the high expectations of the program, Thielman responded, "They hope for a better future."

THE GEORGE LUCAS EDUCATIONAL FOUNDATION

Founded as a nonprofit organization in 1991, the George Lucas Educational Foundation (GLEF) seeks to "celebrate and encourage innovation in schools" (George Lucas Educational Foundation, 2006,
para. 1). George Lucas said, "Teachers are the most important individuals in our society—nothing is as powerful as the human touch in
education" (sidebar). Concerned that too many schools operate in
isolation from their communities and the resources found within
them, Lucas created a foundation that invites educators to be at the
core of innovative work in schools.

Framed around project-based learning, Edutopia provides access to technology and experts that change the essence of learning.
With the belief that technology, global understanding, and social
and emotional learning lie at the heart of education, teachers can
connect students to their futures. Through their online magazine
Edutopia, the foundation documents the "most exciting classrooms" where innovative project-based learning is a mainstay. According to Patricia Harder, National Advisory Board member for
GLEF, "highlighting schools and classrooms is really about analyzing why those schools and classrooms are successful" (interview).

An Interview With Patricia Harder

SW: What is the powerful aspect of GLEF?

PH: I think the foundation has a strong vision of what education can
and should be. That vision breaks the paradigm of traditional schools
and considers an educational model that reflects real life. We talk
about learning taking place outside of school and rethinking school as
a place to share what you learn instead of having learning doled out.
We talk about alternative schedules. What if a child would prefer to

go to school in the afternoon and evening? How do we accommodate that child?

Education has been such a static institution, and we have to change. Look at the physical layout of schools. Classrooms have four walls, an overhead projector, and a desk for each child. But that structure doesn't act like the corporate world or real life. So we're not adequately preparing kids to meet their futures.

The foundation looks beyond these traditional modes of learning and institutionalized settings. It's inspiring.

SW: What have you learned about authentic partnerships through serving on the GLEF advisory board?

PH: It's okay to be untraditional. Traditional models hold no purpose for so many kids.

The foundation looks at project-based learning models that allow students to work with real scientists, with real architects, with experts in the field. These interactions show kids that learning leads somewhere, and they see new value in learning. To be successful, kids have to be able to value their education.

We need to explore new models. When kids work with experts, with real-life people who do real-life jobs, they see passion for learning and understanding. As educators, we have to look at learning in different ways, so more kids can learn.

SW: How does GLEF continue to address the skills students need to be successful in the 21st century?

PH: At GLEF, we are always asking, "What do kids need to know how to do?" It's not just about what they know; it's about what they know how to do.

And listening. We listen a lot. At board meetings, everyone is valued, and we listen to what others have to say. We have a lot of conversation and opportunity for input. Then, we take that information and look at how to transfer the information into the classroom. How do we make change happen?

We also keep a foot in corporate markets. We move with corporations instead of behind them and try to determine how to incorporate those skills into learning experiences for kids. For example, the foundation just created a curriculum for filmmaking as an elective for middle school. It is a project-based learning experience that incorporates writing, life skills, and contemporary literacies. It's not just fluff. It's real learning.

Right now, the foundation is discussing the role of assessment. This is a reality for today's schools and students. We talk about how to align project-based learning experiences to curricular goals, like the filmmaking curriculum, so that kids will master standards necessary to be successful on the state assessments. It's really about deep understanding. We believe that when kids have rich learning experiences that require application and deep understanding, they will be successful with state assessments, too.

GLEF also highlights schools and classrooms that break the paradigm of traditional school. When we do that, we aren't just recognizing them; we are analyzing what they do and how they help all kids to learn. We want to know what makes them successful, and we want to use that information to change education.

SW: What should other educators know about partnering with business?

PH: I think, sometimes, educators suffer from insecurity, and education is often viewed as second class to business. It shouldn't be that way. Educators have a lot to offer in school–business partnerships. Kids have to have skills to be successful in real life. We should always be learning. We should be in constant dialogue (between education and business) so we are moving forward together. When we act confidently to create meaningful partnerships for kids, everyone wins.

SW: What is the hardest aspect of the work GLEF does?

PH: I think it's working to merge education and business rather than to treat them as distinct, separate entities. We need to learn to blend the ideals of both. It's like reading and writing; they are so totally connected, but sometimes, people treat them as completely separate.

SW: What have you learned from serving on the advisory board that transfers into how you work with kids, parents, and the community?

PH: I have more confidence. I also have a vision for what learning can be for my students, and I work toward that vision.

I am constantly networking with places where project-based learning can occur. Even service learning experiences can make a huge difference for my students, allowing them to value their education.

Project-based learning experiences have a deliberate design. While meeting standards, I look at aspects of engagement and differentiation so all students have access and interest. These have to be bona fide learning experiences, or they aren't worth our time.

SW: What is the best aspect of serving on the advisory board?

PH: It broadens my thinking. I am constantly looking at how I can help make this paradigm shift happen. When I create project-based learning experiences for my students, I'm not looking at how much time the project will take or how cute it is. I look at how many curricular goals and standards I can incorporate and how I can use project-based learning to reach different kids.

I also look at new ways to create partnerships and learning experiences in my own community. Right now, I have a child who lives in a really rural area, and her family doesn't go into town that often. So even though "town" isn't that big, it is big to her. I have to find ways to broaden her experiences so she can envision a different future for herself.

Lessons From GLEF   Project-based learning incorporates curricular goals while giving students access to work with and as experts in a field. It provides students with opportunities to apply their learning across disciplines and to demonstrate deep understanding through a project. Such experiences compel students to value their learning because they can see that learning leads somewhere.

Educators have something to contribute in school–business partnerships. These partnerships aren't just about the skills of business; they are about application of skills that students will need throughout life. Students must be able to think about knowledge and apply it in new ways, so the learning that they do everywhere has meaning and application.

Static education models don't work for all kids. We must break traditional paradigms and think about life experiences as the learning—including authentic partnerships—and about school as a place to share that learning. Teachers can no longer be the keepers of all knowledge.

SERVICE LEARNING

A wonderful way to partner with a business while meeting grade-level curricular goals, service learning provides students an opportunity to get a taste of the business world through managing a project and meeting a community need. Unlike straightforward community service, service learning allows students to apply knowledge and skills learned in the classroom to solve real-life problems.

Service learning projects put students in the driver's seat, allowing them to expand their knowledge and hone their skills in an area of interest or current learning. Because students research a need and various ways to address that need, they are challenged to think critically about the series of cause–effect relationships that not only led to the problem but influenced potential solutions.

Make a Difference Day

As probably the most widely known service project, Make a Difference Day, sponsored by the Points of Light Foundation and USA Weekend, is held the fourth Saturday in October. Although groups and persons can get project ideas from the Make a Difference Day website, groups are challenged to design projects to meet community needs.

Numerous national organizations participate, helping to bring the total number of volunteers each year into the millions. Yes, Make a Difference Day may be a one-time community service effort for some. But for most of the participating organizations, including schools, Make a Difference Day allows participants of all ages to delve into issues close to home—to learn about them and to plan a solution and act on it.

COMMON TRAITS

So what do all of these amazing programs have in common? Although they need money and goods to operate, they are not about money and goods; they are about student learning and student achievement. All of these partnerships have curricular goals, but they still leave room for students to make choices and to take ownership of their learning.

Successful partnerships break down old paradigms and work to find the win-win outcome for all parties involved. Thrive by Five addresses early literacy and numeracy skills regardless of where a child spends his or her formative years, breaking down the paradigm that formal education happens in school buildings. By meeting community needs at the root, this program strives to eliminate achievement gaps that plague our nation's schools.

Many of these models seek to serve underserved populations, understanding that when the ocean swells, all boats rise. Although some programs directly state a goal of serving poverty-stricken children, others attempt to pique students' interests and elevate their learning in new models that extend beyond the traditional academic setting. In this way, successful partnerships allow students to invest in their own learning in ways they hadn't previously.

These partnerships and programs don't shy away from high expectations; successful partnerships raise expectations for all students. But because of the experience that authentic partnerships offer, students come prepared to master skills and exceed expectations.

Most important, these partnerships build relationships, connecting to community needs, corporate needs, and academic needs and providing models that allow students to envision a better future for themselves.

KEY IDEAS

A partner is someone who has a stake in your success.
Ultimately, business and education have similar goals—to be successful in a global community and economy.
Successful partnerships have student learning at the core.
Creating meaningful partnerships benefits both business and education.

EDUCATION ADVOCATE ACTION POINTS

Begin today to build meaningful relationships with businesses in your area.
Research model programs.
Work within your school system to align curricular goals to meet the needs of a global community and economy.

QUESTIONS FOR REFLECTION

Which businesses in my community might be interested in partnering on curricular goals to prepare students to be successful in a global community and economy?
Which student groups in my school or school system are currently underserved? How would a school–business partnership serve their needs?
What funding sources could I leverage (including grants) to build school–business partnerships?

6

MONEY, MONEY, MONEY

Maggie sits at her kitchen table on a Saturday looking at the grant applications in front of her. Each one seems so daunting, but her desire to begin an electronic portfolio project with her students consumes her inhibitions about writing a grant proposal. Although her school system considers itself technologically advanced, the one outdated computer in her classroom won't be enough for students to collect evidence of their learning in the way that she envisions.

Her frustration begins to mount as the hours pass and she continues to search websites to find prices for the equipment she will need—computers, software, external CD burners, external hard drives, digital cameras. The beautiful spring day isn't helping her disposition because she would rather be tending to her small garden or hiking with friends—both opportunities she had before she recalled the grant deadlines.

In March, she asked her principal if he could assist with funding for her portfolio project idea. She had even written a brief overview to show how the project would allow students to interact with their own and each other's writing in new, exciting ways. When he indicated that the school's budget couldn't support such a *project, he suggested that Maggie talk to the language arts supervisor at the central office. Although Maggie called her the next day and received full conceptual support, the language arts supervisor explained that the budget would go to the school board in a matter of weeks and that it was too late for a budget initiative for next year. She offered to help Maggie with a budget initiative for the following year, but Maggie was determined to move forward. In light of that information, the language arts supervisor pointed Maggie to several possible grant opportunities to get her started. Now, on a tempting spring Saturday, Maggie sits at her computer.*

Believe it or not, Maggie's situation is not atypical. Often unaware of budget cycles, teachers get behind the curve when it comes to new initiatives for their classrooms. And although grants provide considerable funds for classrooms, they are often time-consuming to write and may not cover the complete project or provide sustainable funds.

It is a sunny Saturday afternoon in the spring and Suzanne, the school system's language arts supervisor, arrives at the office for several hours of work. After taking her kids to dance lessons that morning, she left them at the park with a babysitter so that she could catch up on the week's paperwork.

As Suzanne reviews her e-mail from the week, she notices the reply to a message that she sent Maggie, a teacher in the system, about grant opportunities. She thinks more about how to take Maggie's idea further and to write a budget initiative for the next year's budget cycle. She can easily create a pilot project across all of the system's middle schools. What would that look like? How much hardware and software would be needed? Which teachers might be interested? What training and support would they need? Which funding sources could she tap? Suzanne grabs a file folder and starts to jot down her ideas on paper.

Suzanne knows that she will have several budget initiatives to take to the school board next fall and that this pilot needs some research support if it has any chance of staying in the budget

throughout the budget process. The other initiatives involve stu-
dents in more needy populations than those in Maggie's class, so
that is another item to consider—but a pilot might allow her to ex-
pand the demographics some. Suzanne also knows that a great deal
depends on where previous initiatives are in their funding cycles
and how they have been funded. Local dollars, the premium in the
school system's budget, are difficult to obtain. Can Maggie's proj-
ect qualify for technology funding? How much of that is left?

After jotting down her ideas, Suzanne e-mails her boss the
idea—best to get it on the radar—and continues to check over her
own e-mail.

We all despise budget season, which seems to last the majority
of any school year. Typically, school systems begin the budget
process around October, designing a sort of wish list to continue
current services, provide raises for staff, and account for new initiatives. In some ways, this process begins much like a child's making a list for Santa. Of course, unlike that child, educators know
that a very real conversation will follow, requiring educational leaders to prioritize budget items and propose a budget that will be
close to funding resources. In the spring, school systems work with
their local boards of education to establish and adopt a budget that
falls within budgetary realities while working to advance educational needs and goals. Unfortunately, because federal appropriations and allocations are rarely completed before school systems
must complete their budgetary processes, much of a local budget
gains approval based on the previous year's budget and projections
for revenue.

Believe it or not, this is essentially the same process used at state
and national levels. Unfortunately, most educators don't get involved in the budget process until legislators are preparing to vote
on the budget. In reality, education advocates must involve themselves in the budget process, through discourse with education
stakeholders and legislators, when Congress and state delegations
are making their budget wish lists.

THE FEDERAL BUDGET PROCESS

So, when does the budget process begin on the national level? Believe it or not, federal agencies begin to develop their budgetary needs and requests a full year before the budget will be passed in Congress and a year and a half before the fiscal year. At the federal level, agencies such as the U.S. Department of Education begin analyzing their needs and preparing their requests in May.

In September, federal agencies submit their budget requests to the Office of Management and Budget (OMB), thus beginning the review process and the larger points of negotiation. But at this point, including new initiatives or even requesting that existing initiatives be fully funded may come too late because all of the agencies' requests come together.

Let's take a step back to consider the implications. Education advocates must be thinking 2 years out and discussing their ideas and concerns with legislators if they want their ideas and concerns to carry weight during the budgeting process. It is for this reason that education associations plan long-term agendas and repeatedly share those agendas with decision makers. Much like with the child's list for Santa, the OMB considers each request, prioritizes the list, and makes revisions. By December, various agencies have the recommendations from the OMB and are given an opportunity to appeal those recommendations.

The president's budget request gets drafted to be presented to Congress no later than the first Monday in February, thus ending the formulation phase of the budget process and beginning the congressional process phase. At this point, lobbyists and agencies scramble to respond to the proposed budget—all advocating for their agencies' causes and often using other agencies' allocations to demonstrate shortcomings in the president's budget request.

Between February and April, the budget committees schedule a series of hearings, during which time various departments justify their budget requests and determine appropriations recommendations. Through this process, Congress determines its own plan, called the *budget resolution*, for revenues and spending.

By April 15 of each year, Congress should pass the budget resolution, but that rarely occurs. Thus, the lengthy budget and appropriations process does not usually finish until the late fall, forcing school systems to rely on projections and past allocations to move their own budgets forward. Recent budget issues, the nation's call to balance the budget, and different fiscal years all impede the process.

Additionally, most school systems work on a July-to-June fiscal year, whereas the federal government's fiscal year runs October to September. This discrepancy, coupled with the arduous processes at the federal level, makes accurate budgeting exceptionally difficult.

Getting Involved

What happens in Washington doesn't stay in Washington. What happens in Washington matters. Although getting involved on the national level, especially with the budget, feels like rain drops in the ocean, advocates must speak up for education. To do so, advocates must be involved with their education associations.

National education associations employ people and use their leadership to follow national trends and engage in conversation with members of Congress and their staff on a daily basis. These people are experts in areas of legislation important to their organizations. Through position statements, they provide educators with a breakdown of key points and with a statement on how the proposed budget should change. They research the costs associated with the platforms they support, and they make recommendations throughout the budget and appropriations processes. Advocates can then use this information to make informed decisions and to communicate with their representatives in Congress.

Becoming directly involved with the leadership of an education organization allows individual educators around the nation to be part of a larger voice. Whether at the state or national level, these leader volunteers gather information that, when shared in the greater context, provides the stories and the foundation for the aforementioned position statements and platforms.

Show Us the Money

Thanks to Hollywood and the success of *Jerry McGuire*, anyone with teenagers understands the phrase "Show me the money!" Many parents often feel like their kids always have their hands out. Even with allowances and other family procedures to help teens cover their personal expenses, somehow, it never seems to be enough. Kids always want more, and they see those wants as needs. From the child's perspective, however, a few dollars seem to come with a lot of mandates. Some parents require that their kids put the first 10% of their earnings and allowances in savings, another 10% to a religious or charitable organization, leaving 80% for discretionary expenditures. But even those expenditures have restrictions —paying for one's own entertainment, covering clothing expenses outside of a certain limit, purchasing gifts for friends, and so on. Of course, most parents' intentions are good—this process mimics adult budgeting, and kids learn how to manage money. But the money isn't a gift. It comes with requirements, and most teens would say that the requirements exceed the funds.

A Local Approach

As with money exchanged between teenagers and parents, the same is true of the monies that combine to make a school system's local operating budget—they come with requirements. According to Sturgeon (2006), on a good day, federal dollars account for approximately 8% of a local school system's operating budget. State funding varies but typically contributes an additional 49%. Unfortunately, with No Child Left Behind (NCLB) mandates, the federal government controls approximately 80% of local educational decisions. But a community's citizens, who contribute the bulk of any school system's budget, have the least amount of control in how that budget is allocated.

No successful business would operate a budget in such a manner. Successful businesses know that they must be responsible to their customers first because that is their funding source. Moreover, the stakeholders in a business have the most say in how that company's budget is designed. Private schools use a process that more closely aligns with successful corporations.

In public schools, even though students are the customers, they don't pay a fee for services. As such, the budgetary process becomes more complicated as schools attempt to serve many masters—the students, the taxpayers, and the regulations. In essence, school systems are the teenagers, and the government funding sources are saying, "As long as you live in my house . . . "

A PHILOSOPHICAL STATEMENT

One must bear in mind that a local school system's budget reflects a great deal more than the funds available for any given fiscal year. The budget, in a larger sense, represents the system's philosophy of education and makes a statement about the type of educational programming and priorities that the community, through the school board, will support.

Consider for a moment what each of the following scenarios indicates about underlying educational beliefs:

- To balance the budget, System A eliminates the four central office core coordinator positions, thus allowing raises for teaching personnel and maintaining class sizes below 25

students per class. Consequently, schools no longer have the
curricular support that the central office staff once provided.

- To balance the budget, System B elects not to replace teachers who retire or leave the system, thus allowing all staff who
  have performed adequately to remain in the system if they
  wish. Consequently, several teachers must be transferred to
  meet course offering needs, and class sizes increase.

- To balance the budget, System C reduces elective course offerings, such as the arts and world languages, thus reducing
  the need for instructional staff in these areas. The reduction
  in the arts also reduces the necessary supplies for courses that
  traditionally prove expensive for the school system. Consequently, many teachers in these areas lose their jobs, and
  teachers who remain need to work at multiple schools. Students in this school system may not have access to courses that
  pique their interest and prepare them to participate actively
  in a global community.

- To balance the budget, System D elects to maintain current
  programming and practices but not to add any new initiatives
  in the budget. Increases in revenues will be used to hire any
  needed additional staff based on the full-time-equivalent allocations and to provide cost-of-living raises to all staff. Consequently, the system will not invest in new programs or tech-
  nologies that might reach specific student groups, provide
  avenues for community outreach, and improve working conditions for staff.

Although none of the options are attractive, each one reveals
the school systems' and community's underlying beliefs about
education.

Not only do education advocates recognize that the budget mir-
rors philosophy (with the understanding that the budget provides
a plan for the future), but they also carefully craft the budget to
align with those philosophical beliefs. Working with the commu-

nity and with staff representatives, advocates listen to discern the philosophical underpinnings that should guide the budget process.

UNDERSTANDING THE TERMINOLOGY

To understand the budget process, one must understand the terms associated with creating a budget. Although some of the more basic terms apply to personal budgets as well, thereby making them simple to understand, some terms apply only to business or government situations.

Budgets involve a relatively simple formula: What gets spent must equal or be less than the amount available. Unfortunately, that simple formula doesn't capture the whole picture. As with a child and his or her allowance, the money available may not be the same as the money received. Within the funds available, school officials must be vigilant to appropriately allocate those funds with strings (or restrictions) attached. In short, not all funds act the same.

Local Dollars

No question, local dollars come with the most flexibility. Received through levying taxes or bonds, local funds generally account for between 40% and 45% of a local system's budget (Sturgeon, 2006). Although the state, local government, or local school district sets the tax rate (depending on the state), advocates know that the portion of those taxes allocated for various groups—education, law enforcement, agriculture, and so on—depends greatly on the perceived need in each of those areas. For this reason, educators must convince the greater community that the schools need the funding and that the school system will spend those funds appropriately. And, sometimes, advocates must uncover and respond to deeper issues.

An Example   In one community where I worked, we desperately needed to build a new high school to replace an existing campus of older buildings. A significant increase in student population had the facility splitting at the seams. More than 20 trailers littered the parking lots. Time had taken its toll on the original building, and added buildings no longer supported instructional needs. With the rise in technology, rewiring the buildings was not a viable option. Moreover, overall renovation would have proved nearly as costly as a new facility. Although the county already owned the land, taxpayers fought against passing the bond for several years.

Although the school system presented an accurate and compelling case, work to uncover additional issues hadn't been done. Specifically, citizens in this area of the county had voted for bonds to build additional facilities in other areas of the county as growth occurred. So, at this point in time, the majority of students were attending school in new buildings, and their parents weren't convinced that a new school was necessary. In short, their children's schools were new, and they were paying taxes to cover those bonds—why add another one? Also, this school sat in the least transient part of the county, and many of the taxpayers in the immediate area had attended school in the original building. Emotional attachments held people back. Finally, although the educators understood the need to accommodate technological advancements, the majority of the taxpayers didn't own computers and didn't appreciate the need or understand the associated costs.

Once administrators in the school system understood these needs, they were able to become better advocates. Partnering with teachers, parents, business leaders, and students, the administration pulled more people into the process of communicating with voters. Demonstrating an appreciation for tradition and taking care to fully explain, through formal and informal communications, the reasons behind the needs, they were finally able to pass the bond referendum.

So, although local dollars carry the most flexibility into the budgeting process, they must be accounted for with the community at large. Unfortunately, because government support for legislation has not reached original commitment levels, local dollars often get tapped to meet state and federal mandates.

Federal Dollars

Despite often being in short supply, federal dollars carry the most restrictions. Title I funds, for example, may be spent only for Title I services. Special education funds must be spent on special education. Moreover, systems must report not only fund expenditures but also program evaluations demonstrating student growth. As previously mentioned, federal dollars account for approximately 8% of a local school system's operating budget.

Debts and Deficits

School officials design local budgets around various funding sources, including state and federal dollars. But to drive home how little the federal government contributes to that local budget, one must understand the difference between debts and deficits. Most of us are familiar with debt—money that we owe and must repay. Currently, the national debt is around $9 trillion. To get the full effect of that number, let's insert all of those zeros— $9,000,000,000,000! That's money that the U.S. government owes someone.

The deficit, however, is actually a much more interesting concept. This is the amount of money that the federal government spent beyond revenues in a single year. In the fiscal year (FY) 2007 budget, that number is $423 billion. Even more compelling to educators, though, is that the entire FY 2007 budget request for discretionary funds for all major domestic areas, including education, health and human services, agriculture, and so on (not mandatory items, such as social security or environmental protection) is less than the deficit. In short, according to the FY 2007 federal budget, the government can exceed revenues by more money than what is allocated for all major nonmandatory domestic programs combined.

Authorization Versus Appropriation

Even more disturbing than the fact that the deficit may exceed funds for all major domestic areas, the federal budget allocations for major education programs such as the Individuals With Disabilities Education Act (IDEA) and Title I generally reflect half (or less) of the authorized amount.

Like debt versus deficit, authorization versus appropriation takes educators by surprise. The authorized amount represents how much a certain program will cost to operate. For example, in FY 2007, the authorized level for Title I programs is $25 billion, although the president's budget calls for only $12.7 billion to be appropriated for Title I programs. The appropriated amount can range anywhere from zero to the authorized level. In short, this is the amount allocated for a specific area or piece of legislation.

Again, let's look at this from a more local perspective. A local school board may authorize the mathematics coordinator to spend $300,000 on new textbooks for students in grades K–12. It did not, however, authorize her to spend that money needlessly or unwisely. Bearing in mind that each of those dollars comes from levying taxes and from wanting to be responsible with taxpayer money, the coordinator negotiates the best deal possible for the best textbook to meet the school system's overall curricular goals in mathematics. In the end, she spends $250,000, leaving $50,000 available for other school system resources. In the next fiscal year, the school board may authorize $300,000 for new learning resources but only appropriate $250,000 of that based on the previous year's expenditures. In doing so, they are making a statement that they expect actual spending to be at that level.

Why not just appropriate the authorized amount? Although the government may allow spending beyond its resources (deficit) in a fiscal year, appropriating every area at authorized levels would lead to outrageous spending allocations. Unfortunately, every department believes that its area of responsibility should be funded at maximum levels, at which point Congress must make choices. However, budgetary restraints mustn't prevent educators from explaining to Congress the need for full funding, fully expecting that the government will hold true to the promises made through the legislative process.

Encumbered Versus Unspent Funds

Imagine it's payday. Yay! On payday, X amount of money gets deposited into your checking account. Now imagine that you want to buy a new television and you go to the store with the total of your paycheck still in your account. Do you really have that much unspent money? Of course not. If you were to spend all of the money in your account on a television, it's likely that you wouldn't be able to pay your mortgage or rent, utilities, and other bills. So even though the money is there, technically, it has already been encumbered to account for bills for which you already know that you have obligations. Moreover, only the unwise would actually spend every penny, assuming that the same paycheck would be there, like clockwork, during the next pay cycle. The same holds true for any budget, including that of education.

Unfortunately, staffers in legislators' offices and the press often hear about or read that school systems do not spend all of the money allocated in a given year, thereby deducing that education is well funded if money is still available. Untrue. School systems do not get a lump sum on July 1 and spend wisely throughout the year. On the contrary, the government reimburses school systems, usually monthly, for the expenses that they have already incurred. So, as with your personal account, it would be unwise to spend every penny, lest an emergency arise. Still, according to the Committee for Education Funding (2006), "the $66 million returned to the Treasury as unspent in 2004 represents about one tenth of one percent (0.1%) of the FY04 education funds. In other words, 99.9% of the money Congress allocated was spent."

In addition to wise spending practices, another reason that some funds may actually be left unspent is that of regulations placed on them. During my last visit to Capitol Hill, one staffer asked directly about funds that had been unspent, even returned, from my home state. When I inquired as to which funds she was referring, I learned that they were federal monies for Title I that were restricted to staff development. What I explained was that although systems actively worked to expend those monies, restrictions against using the funds for travel related to staff development impeded some systems' abilities to use the funds in a given year. If, for example, a staff development workshop cost $150 for a staff member to attend but that travel would cost another $150, the school system, depending on policy, may need to match the government funds.

Budget Cuts and Level Funding

As I write, the House of Representatives is proposing its FY 2007 budget (for the 2007–2008 school year). If they follow President Bush's recommendations, education will take two hits—one, budget cuts to specific programs and, two, level funding, which translates into a budget cut. Educators must understand how each of these recommendations translates into decreased funding for education.

Budget cuts are fairly self-explanatory. In essence, we currently allocate X amount to a specific program; a budget cut recommends $X-x$ for that program or even eliminates the program altogether.

President Bush's FY 2007 proposal eliminates 42 programs and cuts funding to many others. Of course, some of these programs have been absorbed into larger areas of the budget, and some may now be obsolete, but the overall budget for education was proposed for the largest cut in the history of the U.S. Department of Education, 3.8%.

Below the surface, programmatic budget cuts often affect the neediest student populations. Thus, to continue to serve these students, school systems must allocate local dollars to continue to support effective programs. In this way, programs aside from those directly stated in the budgetary process lose funding because monies are shifted to continue services.

The most notable examples of this type of cut occur in special education and Title I. In President Bush's proposed budget for FY 2007, Title I funding remains more than $12 billion below the authorized level, and IDEA remains more than $6 billion below its authorized level and $15 billion below full funding as promised by Congress. These programs in particular not only reach the nation's neediest students but also carry the most stringent restrictions on spending. Moreover, these programs have been consistently underfunded by approximately 50% or more over the last decade (see Appendix B).

Much like the deeper-rooted issues with programmatic budget cuts, across-the-board cuts don't reduce funding equally across student populations. As seen in the previous segment, 2006–2007 proposed Title I program cuts directly affect both Title I students and regular education students. Layering on an additional 3% across-the-board cut affects local school systems by making it more difficult to continue the previous year's level of services for all student populations. And because federally regulated programs mandate levels of funding and staffing, that across-the-board cut most seriously affects regular instruction and staffing for regular instruction.

Nonnegotiable Versus Discretionary Dollars

Even more disturbing in the overall budget process than the outwardly stated funding recommendations are the hidden ways in which schools lose the ability to leverage dollars for instructional purposes. This essentially works like a personal budget, leveraging nonnegotiable and discretionary dollars to meet a school division's needs.

In my personal budget, for example, I must account first for nonnegotiable expenses. These are items such as my mortgage, car payment, utilities, clothing, and food. In today's banking system, nonnegotiable budget items are often directly transferred from a checking or savings account to the payee. Although I could opt not to pay these bills, such a choice would eliminate functional aspects of my life. In essence, without these items, I cannot survive sufficiently.

In the same way, school systems have nonnegotiable items in their budgets. These expenses might include capital outlay, transportation, and utilities. These items must be accounted for on a monthly basis. Much like those in my personal budget, without these expenditures, the functional aspects of school would cease to exist.

In my personal budget, discretionary dollars are those monies that I use for items of choice. In some ways, these items may overlap or supplement nonnegotiable expenses. I must wear clothes to work. However, nothing in the dress code indicates that I must buy my suits from Talbots. Likewise, I must eat to survive, but I do not need to eat lobster and steak every day. In my personal budget, discretionary monies also cover entertainment expenses, books, travel, haircuts, and so on. The big idea is not that all of these items are truly optional but that they require choice and prioritization.

In a school system's budget, staff, learning resources, and programs are not optional, but the extent to which we leverage funds for them and the choices that we make within those areas require choice and prioritization. Sadly, most boards of education would like to allocate not only substantial monies (that already happens because the largest expenditure in a local budget is staff) but sufficient monies to cover these non-optional but discretionary areas.

HOW UNDERFUNDED MANDATES ULTIMATELY AFFECT SCHOOLS—A LOCAL EXAMPLE

So, how are schools affected? Albemarle County, Virginia, covers an enormous area—726 square miles, or 465,040 acres. The county school system serves approximately 12,500 students each year. The school system's 218 busses travel approximately 10,000 miles each day to transport students to and from school (Albemarle County Public Schools, 2006). Since 2001, energy costs have more than doubled, and although the student population has steadily increased, transportation routes have not changed a great deal. So, to transport students to and from school today costs more than twice what it did just 4 years ago. Transporting students and the associated energy costs are nonnegotiable expenditures.

In that same period, the federal government, as seen in the graph in Appendix B, has steadily decreased funding for education. The Commonwealth of Virginia has counterbalanced these cuts to some degree, increasing state funding. However, in 2005–2006, the local government decreased funding to schools, and transportation costs have doubled. Consequently, fewer dollars are available for discretionary purposes—that is, instruction.

A WORD ABOUT GRANTS

One avenue that local school systems take to supplement funding available for instruction is to apply for and receive grant monies. With values ranging from a few hundred dollars to hundreds of thousands of dollars, grants provide a reasonable means for implementing new programs, providing staff development around an instructional practice, securing staffing for targeted areas, and purchasing learning resources. Grants are wonderful, but they are not without a downside. Grant monies come in finite amounts and for finite periods.

When applying for grants, educators must work together to target areas of concern and to ensure that, once grant monies are exhausted, new programs or staffing can be maintained. Never, ever rely on grant extensions to support continued efforts. If the grant money will supplement a critical area, forward thinking regarding the local budget can ensure that students get the resources that they need in order to learn.

Additionally, educators must consider the implications of receiving grant monies. If, for example, a technology grant allows a school to purchase 100 computers to outfit new labs, but the building's wiring is 50 years old, to use the grant monies, the school may need to ante up the funds to rewire the building to support the new technology. At first glance, the new computers sound great, but the additional costs may exceed the benefits, especially if they come as a surprise.

Educators must also bear in mind that grants are not free money. Federal grants in particular carry significant restrictions as to how funds may be used. Even grants from individual corporations may specify unrealistic timelines or product restrictions. Researching the limitations of the grant before applying allows educators to plan realistically for new initiatives and to sustain existing ones.

SPEAK UP!

Educators must write to their representatives requesting full funding of education requirements. As mentioned in previous chapters, the federal government has yet to reach its funding commitments for NCLB and IDEA, and it has reduced funding for critical programs, such as Title I. Educators must raise their voices and demonstrate to leaders that level funding and budget cuts directly affect the local budgetary process and—much, much more important—the students.

KEY IDEAS

Education advocates must work to influence local budgets from the onset, at the more conceptual point in the process.

Education advocates must work to influence the federal budget process by working with their education associations and by writing to members of Congress, encouraging them to fully fund education programs.

On a good day, federal dollars account for approximately 8% of a local school system's operating budget.

Budget cuts for some students always affect all students.

All budgets include nonnegotiable and discretionary expenditures. Education advocates must influence legislators to leverage sufficient funds to cover both.

To balance budgets, people (be it personal or organizational) prioritize and ultimately cut discretionary monies.

Grants provide one means for supplementing local budgets.

EDUCATION ADVOCATE ACTION POINTS

Learn about and become involved with the entire budgetary process at local, state, and federal levels.

Encourage legislators to fully fund initiatives and provide for sustained funding for the life of the requirement.

Fight against budget proposals that cut funding for education.

Investigate grant options that provide initial monies and carry potential for sustainable business partnerships.

QUESTIONS FOR REFLECTION

How do I see federal funding affecting classrooms in my school
or school system?

Which programs are most at risk when the federal government
doesn't fully fund education mandates?

What philosophical statement does my school system's budget
make? Which items in the budget support my belief?

In what ways have budget cuts and level funding hurt or elimi-
nated programs needed to meet students' learning needs?

7

BRANCHING OUT: STATE AND FEDERAL CONVERSATIONS

Since attending a recent conference, James has become more disheartened with education policy. It seems that every time the budget gets tight, his urban school and its students get the short end of the stick. Programs that build technical skills and support his students' interests and career goals receive fewer and fewer funds.

At school, James gathers a group of fellow educators to discuss the implications of state and federal mandates and budget cuts. Although frustrated, they want to take action, but they don't know what to do. No one in the group has time to visit Washington; they have students to teach.

What was wrong with these people in Washington anyway? Didn't anyone there talk to educators in the field before making decisions?

Really, James would like to close his door and teach, but "those people" were making it impossible.

◦ ◦ ◦

Julie, a member of many education associations and a board member for a state organization, sits at her computer catching up on e-mail. It is after hours, and her office is finally quiet, making this *an ideal time to think. She notices an e-mail from Leslie, a staffer in the Senate. Clicking on it, she thinks about the last time that she and Leslie talked.*

It was just last month, Julie thought, glancing down at the brief message requesting information about preK programs in her school system. The senator needs local stories and data for a meeting on Friday—and this was Tuesday. A high school principal, Julie wasn't sure about the information; she would have to track it down. Thankfully, she was meeting one of the elementary principals for dinner, so that would be a start.

Hitting the reply button, Julie scripts a quick return message, indicating that she received the e-mail and needed some time to gather the information. She would make every effort to have the requested information in the next 2 days. Even if she doesn't get everything, Julie knows that providing as much accurate information as she could would continue the healthy relationship that she has with this staffer and allow her to not only influence the senator's position but possibly help shape future legislation.

Turning to her calendar, Julie makes two notes: On Wednesday, follow up with preK information and send it to Leslie; on Monday, call Leslie to see if there was anything else that the senator needed on preK and remind her that she would like to know about developments with high school reform legislation.

Some educators perceive the state and federal legislatures as a daunting place to engage in a conversation—especially, one about education. They believe that if they can make a difference in their own communities, then that's enough. It's not. State and federal regulations extend across local boundaries and must be addressed in the best interest of all.

EACH-VERSUS-ALL LEGISLATION

At state and federal levels, there exist essentially two types of educational legislation—legislation for all children and legislation for each child (Rhodes & Deming, 2004). Each type seeks to guarantee a specific outcome, so educators must understand the language used.

When elected officials campaign, doesn't it make sense that they design plans that affect all children? Would you vote for an official who was proposing an education plan supporting the notion that only some children could learn? Probably not. In fact, our nation instituted compulsory education laws to require that all children be afforded some type of education. But legislation that affects all children, to date, neglects to distinguish among various needs in student populations.

The No Child Left Behind Act

The most current, most powerful piece of legislation that affects all children is the No Child Left Behind Act of 2001 (NCLB). In this articulation, the government seeks to guarantee a minimal set of standards for every child in the nation—regardless of socioeconomic status, ethnicity, language acquisition, special needs, and so on. Educational leaders are well aware of the subpopulations that count in their respective school systems and schools. Specifically, the legislation stipulates that it is an act "to close the achievement gap with accountability, flexibility, and choice, so that no child is left behind."

Achievement Gap   The primary issue that NCLB seeks to address involves the gap in achievement, as stated in the act, for so-called disadvantaged students. The language continues on to state that all children should have equal opportunity to reach "at minimum, proficiency on challenging state academic achievement standards and state academic assessments." Right there, advocates should take pause. No one wants his or her child to achieve the minimum. Beyond that, individual states will determine the standards and the assessments that indicate minimum proficiency—not groups of states, not the nation, but individual states. And although education is a state entity, NCLB places the full burden of creating,

implementing, and evaluating proficiency standards and assessments on the state. There is nothing in NCLB to ensure consistency
across the nation or to actually (and fully) close the achievement gap,
thereby bringing all students to approximately the same level of
learning—rather, it ensures just a standard of minimal proficiency.

Accountability   By 2014, under NCLB, school systems must
eliminate gaps in achievement for all children. To accomplish this,
schools must demonstrate that their students are making adequate
yearly progress (AYP) toward the goal of eliminating the achievement gap. Students must take assessments in reading and mathematics in grades 3 through 8 and at least once in high school, and
at least 95% of all students must be assessed. Schools that do not
make AYP incur sanctions that may lead to public-school-of-choice
options for parents and, ultimately, to school closure. But there is
nothing in the current act that rewards schools for making significant gains toward this goal. There is nothing in the current act that
considers the significant needs of schools in highly transient areas
or the needs of specific student populations. And there is nothing
in the current act that accounts for student learning in relation to
a national definition of proficiency.

Moreover, the National Parent–Teacher Association, the National Education Association, the Association for Supervision and
Curriculum Development, the American Educational Research
Association, and numerous other education associations believe
that relying on a single measure to determine student achievement
constitutes bad practice. Because of assessment and accountability
requirements under NCLB, most citizens now believe that assessment is synonymous with standardized testing. What educators
know is that assessment includes everything that a child says, does,
doesn't say, and doesn't do. In short, in every single interaction
with a child, a professional educator gathers some piece of information that reveals what a child understands and is able to do. No
single measure accounts for the complexity of learning.

Flexibility and Choice   Although NCLB attempts to offer more flexibility in how federal dollars are spent at the state and local levels, the federal portion of the local budget remains so seriously underfunded that school systems still struggle to fund needed initiatives to meet requirements under NCLB. When schools do not make AYP and incur sanctions, not only do they have less flexibility with federal dollars, because set amounts must be allocated for staff development and specific programs, but the sanctions themselves cost money.

Imagine that School A serves 500 students who live in an area encircling the school. The next-closest schools, B and C, are each 10 miles from School A, each in different directions. Now, imagine that School A fails to make AYP in 3 consecutive years, and, according to NCLB, parents must be afforded another schooling option for their students. The school system offers up Schools B and C as alternatives, and each school receives 100 students from School A.

What are the implications? Transportation. Staffing. Class size. Programming. Overcrowding. Every area of the life of the schools involved will be affected. Additionally, with these sanctions, the federal government has made the assumption that Schools B and C are necessarily better than School A, as reported through their data. NCLB doesn't account for natural variances in school population that necessarily change when parents elect school of choice options. Although it is possible that scores (and learning?) could improve at all three locations, the possibility also exists that scores will go down.

Just as one teacher isn't responsible for all of an individual child's learning, neither is a single school. Even if the child has not transferred from one school to another, environmental factors—significantly, including early literacy instruction—account for a large portion of a child's overall learning and achievement.

What Next   Although NCLB is fundamentally flawed, no one argues that it has made what was once invisible, visible. Children who remained veiled behind overall statistics that hide more than they reveal have unmasked themselves and their learning needs.

NCLB is due for reauthorization in 2007. With that, education associations and educator advocates will call on Congress to reform NCLB to focus on and support success rather than remain entirely punitive in nature. Additionally, full funding to support state development of "growth model" assessment systems, preK, smaller class size, and teacher recruitment and retention, including staff development, will be necessary.

The Individuals With Disabilities Education Act

The Individuals With Disabilities Education Act (IDEA), a prime example of each-child legislation, seeks to guarantee an appropriate education for each individual child. In this way, legislators respond to various students' needs and call on educators to differentiate instruction to meet those student-specific needs.

Specifically, the act reads that "education of children with disabilities can be made more effective by . . . ensuring their [students with disabilities'] access to the general curriculum in the regular classroom, to the maximum extent possible" and by "providing appropriate special education and related services, and aids and supports in the regular classroom, to such children, whenever appropriate." The act continues on to acknowledge the different learning needs of children in an increasingly diverse population.

IDEA is the only act that requires a free appropriate public education. Surprised? According to Terry Dozier, teacher in residence under secretary of education Richard W. Riley, the only children who are guaranteed a free appropriate public education are those who qualify for special education services. The rest of education gets wrapped into NCLB, a law that doesn't address individual students' needs.

So, why should educators care about all- and each-child legislation? Quite simply, educators tend to work from the each-child perspective. Our pedagogy tells us that each child matters. It is for this reason that most educators get a little bent out of shape over standardized assessments—particularly, the practice of using one assessment to measure what students know and understand about a subject. However, most educational leaders recognize the benefit of assessing all students because of the simple fact that what gets tested gets noticed. In this way, all-child legislation forces those inside and outside of education to notice the needs of each child.

SPEAKING UP IN WASHINGTON

Having your voice heard in Washington takes effort. According to the Congressional Management Foundation (2005), communications with Congress have increased 400% in the last decade (1995–2005), with Congress receiving in excess of 200 million communications in 2004. The expediency of e-mail and the Internet make communicating with members accessible and relatively easy. Unfortunately, during that same decade, congressional staffing did not increase, so staffers handle more communications each day. Today, instead of being one of thousands of voices vying for attention on the Hill, expect to be one of millions.

Timeliness Matters

Understanding the legislative process and getting involved early in that process allows more opportunity for contact and flow of information with officials in Washington. Unfortunately, as demonstrated in the budget section, too many people wait until a piece of legislation is up for a vote (or until it isn't getting funded) before they get involved. Voicing your ideas while a bill is in its formative stage presents a greater chance that those ideas will translate into shaping the bill itself.

Meeting with legislators between sessions when they are in their districts provides the greatest likelihood that your concerns will be heard and translated into action. This is the time when legislators are connecting with the people and gathering information from the home front that will influence their committee work and votes once they return to Washington.

Consider this. When are you most likely to hear your constituents' concerns? Unless an absolute emergency arises, I never present new information or ideas to the superintendent as she heads into a board meeting, or as she runs between meetings, or as she is headed out the door to go home. Either I schedule an appointment, preferably during a school holiday when she is still working, or I allow her to come to me after a brief correspondence. Why? Quite simply, she will be more open to new ideas and information when she doesn't feel rushed.

The same holds true for our elected officials. When in Washington, they and their staff run between meetings and votes. Also, during this time, lobbyists, action committees, representatives from professional organizations, and constituents visiting the Capitol all request a piece of their time to get their issues on the record. But when legislators return to their districts, they aren't quite so rushed, although they are still technically working. They have more time to hear the stories and issues that their constituents want to share. In short, this is when they have come to you.

Once the bill has been drafted, wait until it has been introduced to contact legislators representing your district. If the bill isn't listed in the computer system, staffers will be unable to check its status and to respond appropriately to your concerns. But don't wait too long. It takes time for staffers to research alternate positions on an issue. If you want to affect a member's vote, you need to be in contact at least a week before the vote is taken both in the committee and by the full House or Senate. Additionally, know if your member is on the appropriations committee and, if so, take measures to communicate the funding needs for education programs.

The Right Contact   Contacting the appropriate congressional office not only saves time and effort but also indicates that you understand the legislative process. Although related, the Senate and House are different entities, and they don't vote on each other's legislation. Writing to a senator about a piece of legislation in the House only serves to irritate staff.

Before contacting a congressional office, research the member's position on the issue. Bombarding a member's office with e-mail and petitions if the member already agrees with you wastes resources on all fronts. Instead, target those members who need persuading, providing the key information needed for them to reconsider their stance. Ensuring that communications acknowledge the member's position on an issue allows staffers to expedite his or her actions.

Know the Staffers

When I survey groups of educators, most of them believe that the most important person or people whom they could know in the state or federal government is their district's representative or representatives. Wrong. It would be nice to build up personal relationships with each of those individuals, but it is extremely difficult and often unnecessary. To an educational leader, the most important person in Washington is the congress member's staffer on education.

Who is the average staffer? Unless the member serves on an education committee, his or her education staffer probably handles multiple areas of legislation. He or she most likely mimics the following profile:

Age: mid-20s
Educational background: political science
Last time in a K–12 school: the day before high school graduation
Interest in education as an entity: to cover the facts while pursuing a more prestigious staff position

Knowledge of educational issues: minimal
Knowledge of the legislative process: excellent
Tenure in position: 1–2 years

So why do you want to build a relationship with staffers? They write the summaries of pieces of legislation on which the member will vote. Because their expertise is not likely to be in the field of education, it is imperative that educational leaders build relationships as a means to leverage their expertise. Once that relationship is established, each time that the member has a question about legislation, the staffer will call to field the question and gain information. In this way, educational leaders can have significant influence not only on members' votes but also on the crafting of the legislation itself.

How does this look in action? Forty-eight hours before an educational piece of legislation comes up for vote, a document is delivered to each member's office. Before the package arrives, committee members, other congressional leaders, and lobbyists have been engaged in conversation to leverage the vote, and they generally have a pretty clear idea about how that vote will look. So, once the actual document is delivered, the staffer writes a summary that addresses key points, thus allowing the member to make a decision on how to vote. If, however, the staffer has a question about an aspect of the legislation, he or she needs someone in the field to call. In short, you want to be that person.

But even before the piece of legislation is delivered, congressional leaders negotiate with one another and with lobbyists to craft the legislation. Often, the phrasing of key terms becomes critical to moving the legislation forward. Again, you want a call from that staffer who is advising the member on how to proceed. Getting the educator's perspective early in the process ensures that the piece of legislation is education friendly.

Also significant, that twenty-something staffer carries expertise in an area that you probably don't—the legislative process and, more important, his or her boss. Staffers know the pieces of legislation that hold the member's interest and how she or he will likely vote. Some staffers are more candid than others, but working with them often provides insight for you as an advocate.

During a recent trip to the Hill, I met with several staffers in both the Senate and House offices. Although warmly received in all, one staffer made it clear that his boss's focus for the new session would be on reauthorizing NCLB, not on making changes in regards to the FY 2007 budget, promoting a whole-child approach to education, or investigating high school reform. Although I disagreed with much of what this staffer said about his boss's position, that information allowed me to adjust my communication and efforts with this office.

Another staffer indicated that her boss intended to make education his top priority in the new session and requested information beyond the ASK briefs that our group had already provided. Working together, we were able to follow up with this staffer, knowing that our efforts to gather data and stories from the field would be used to support our positions.

Know Their Records, Committees, and Interests

Whether you agree or disagree with elected officials, demonstrating respect for their positions and interests will prove more effective than not. Consider your own response to a child who says "Yuck!" versus one who says "No, thank you." Moreover, attempting to understand an issue from multiple perspectives affords new insights into the intricacies of a bill and its crafting.

Knowing how various members vote allows advocates to tap into trends and undercurrents that may affect their message. For example, acknowledging that a member's voting record has consistently mirrored the interests of education indicates to the member that you have done the appropriate research and that the ASK being presented likely aligns with his or her own beliefs. However, learning that farmland composes the majority of a member's district and recognizing that keeping farmers afloat may require more of his or her attention allows you to highlight the key information that the member must know to support education.

Likewise, knowing on which committees members serve helps to frame an ASK tailored to their interests and abilities to act. Just as a principal doesn't handle every discipline issue in a large high school, legislators do not address every piece of legislation. Instead, a member's staff focuses on the pieces of legislation related to the member's committee or committees and those items that will be presented to the entire House or Senate.

Moreover, congressional offices receive thousands of communications each day on just about every topic under the sun. Tailoring the message to meet education's needs and to target a legislator's interests and reasonable capabilities creates a win-win situation.

Writing to Legislators—Key Components

Writing to legislators typically causes some anxiety. After all, these are powerful elected officials. And with all the mail and other papers, you might wonder if your letter will even be read or responded to. According to Dozier, who spoke to a group of National Board certified teachers about this topic, it takes only nine letters on a specific issue to persuade a member to reconsider or solidify his or her vote on an issue. That's it. Sadly, considering all of the educators across this nation, most of whom do not take this important step to influence education legislation, most members do not receive any correspondence on educational issues. It's time that they did.

So, you've decided that it's time to write to one of your delegates or congressional leaders. What should you say? How should you begin? How much detail should you include? Relax. Remember that as an educational leader, you are the expert in the field. That said, some key components in writing to legislators ought to be considered.

First, write with a specific purpose in mind. For example, in March 2006, I wrote a letter to the representative for my district to encourage him to support in the House of Representatives the budgetary recommendations already passed in the Senate (see Appendix C). Those recommendations included adding $7 billion to fund education, health, and workforce training and $2 billion in additional funding for IDEA. My purpose was clear, and in that letter, I never deviated from the need of the House of Representatives supporting those funding levels.

Second, offer solutions. In the previous situation, the Senate actually offered the solution, so all I needed to do was reiterate it. Often, national organizations will offer a solution as well, so the more informed you are on the issues, the clearer such solutions will become.

Let's draw out an example presented in the previous chapter. You give your teenager an allowance and expect that she or he will maintain a budget within that allowance while adhering to your parameters for expenditures and saving. Unfortunately, your child always seems to be running short on cash. If she or he comes to you and asks for more cash, you feel used, and if this happens repeatedly, you will probably become aggravated and feel sapped. However, if that same teenager suggests a solution, you will likely be much more open to discussing the issue at hand and more likely to assist when a reasonable solution has been placed on the table. In this instance, perhaps, the teenager suggests that she or he be allowed to break curfew once a week to baby-sit for the kids down the street. Although you may negotiate the logistics and look for alternative solutions that don't involve breaking curfew, you are now engaged in discussing the issue and seeking out new solutions. In short, Congress works the same way.

Finally, showcase how the issue directly affects students and staff, without being sappy or overly emotional. It won't get you anywhere to show a picture of poor little Janie in the third grade who doesn't have any prayer of passing standardized assessments because she has a stressful home life, came to school with serious language deficits, and has suffered emotional trauma. Janie is exactly one nonvoting minor in the legislator's arena of constituents. However, highlighting that 500 students in a Title I elementary school will lose two staff members and countless learning resources will get you somewhere.

The following list includes other considerations when writing to legislators:

Write to delegates and congressional leaders in your district. Your spouse's cousin's husband's sister doesn't matter nearly as much to you as your spouse. Likewise, legislators respond to their constituents.

Use an appropriate salutation to show respect. I currently work with a teacher who insists on referring to me as "sister." Honestly, it puts me out at the beginning of every conversation with this individual and keeps me at bay each time that he uses it within the conversation. Appropriate salutations for legislators are included in Appendix D.

Be brief. Stay on message and don't meander.

Know how your member has voted. If the member has been a consistent supporter of education, acknowledging that voting record shows the member that you pay attention not just to your own school's needs but to the larger picture. Members' votes are available on various government websites (see Appendix E).

Include factual student- and staff-centered information. Exaggerating an issue will always come back to haunt you.

Send an original letter; don't send a form letter or a form e-mail. Just like your junk mail at home, they end up in the trash can.

Fax or e-mail your letters to reach your federal representatives. Written mail is often delayed for weeks in the screening process.

Meeting With Legislators—Key Components

Although the key communication points from writing to legislators apply to meeting with them, advocates should consider some additional points.

Although it may be exciting to meet directly with the member of Congress, it's an unlikely event. During their time in Washington, members spend their days in committee meetings and work sessions negotiating pieces of legislation. Decisions on bills for which they do not have direct responsibility are based on information from staffers, which is presented in sound bites and key points. As such, meeting with a staffer who spends his or her time researching and reviewing education policy and meeting with educators often provides more opportunity for continued input than does meeting with the member.

It surprises most people to learn that the actual writing of a piece of legislation is a largely bipartisan process. Everyone wants to do the right thing—in this case, provide the best education possible for America's youth. According to Kelly Scott (2006), former education policy advisor for the Subcommittee on Education and Early Childhood Development, partisan politics aren't likely to affect legislation until the piece has been drafted and presented to the members for vote. Additionally, staffers across the aisle work closely together and generally like each other—even if they disagree on certain positions. Staffers within an office are in constant communication to keep each other abreast of issues and constituent concerns, thus allowing them to better serve the member.

That said, educator advocates should perceive meetings on the Hill as ways to engage in an ongoing conversation in which everyone has the same goal. The educator brings to the table perspective and local stories to support specific views on legislation.

Educators should do the following in a face-to-face meeting:

Be concise. Show consideration of staff time. You ought to be able to get your message across in 6 minutes.

Know your audience. In this case, the member of Congress. What is the member's voting record? On which committees does the member serve? Recognize that the members of Congress must keep in mind a national perspective while responding to concerns of constituents at home.

Identify a key person in your group and one in the member's office as points of contact. Because staffers work so closely, it is more important to maintain a positive relationship than to get to the right person.

Limit your conversation to two or three topics. If you leave materials with the staffer or member, be sure that the materials are concise one-page briefs and that the information contains a website link for your school district or organization.

Provide factual information. If you don't have the answer to a question, get back to the staffer with the correct information.

Identify an ASK. That is, identify what you want done.

Offer to be a resource. Ask what you can do to help the member or staffer as he or she works on the issue at hand.

Show respect. Even if you disagree on issues.

Send a thank you e-mail. A courtesy that spans all arenas.

Keep yourself on the radar. Keep staff informed of changes through e-mail.

INVITING THE OUTSIDE IN

Another key way to gain access to state and federal legislators is, quite simply, to invite them into the schools. Yes, many invitations are declined, but when a legislator seeks out an opportunity to visit schools, wouldn't you want your school system to be at the top of the list?

Not all invitations are declined, however. In those instances, be prepared to show your school and school system in the best light possible and include on the tour classrooms that emphasize the diverse aspects of education.

According to the Learning First Alliance (2005) in their publication *A Practical Guide to Promoting America's Public Schools*, Americans "share deeply held values about, and a common vision for, their public schools" (p. 1). The alliance continues on to indicate that those values should be at the heart of promoting education; values such as the American dream, opportunity, equal access, and safety stand out as a shared vision. In essence, Americans want to see their schools as those promoting responsible citizenship and access for all kids. This should be the core of any tour with public officials. If you don't know what the constituents want, how will you showcase it?

On a tour, demonstrate the ways in which your schools are safe, without shutting out community members. If, for example, visitors to your school wear a badge, politely ask each member of the visiting team to wear a badge as well. They won't be offended; they will be pleased to see procedures in place to protect children.

Emphasize that you provide high-quality instruction, and escort visitors to classrooms in core areas of instruction—English-language arts, mathematics, history and social sciences, and science. Allow visitors to see the teachers and programs that teach students reading, writing, and arithmetic. But beyond that, emphasize, too, that today's children must be able to compete in a global community, and stress how those programs and skills prepare students for success in life, not just in academics.

Take the group to a health or physical education class. Health care issues dominate many conversations in Washington, and the rising cost of health care, especially for children, creates a compound problem inside and outside of schools. Showcase activity that promotes lifelong dedication to fitness and health.

If you have other amazing programs—the arts, an elective stemming from the core, advanced placement, international baccalaureate, career and technical education—visit those classrooms and discuss how those programs benefit students. Be sure to include the level of access for all students and how those programs push kids to excel in specific areas. If the programs reach out to the community, address that as well.

Finally—and this is admittedly a bias of mine—show the visiting team the library. It doesn't take a soothsayer to predict that reading will remain a hot topic in education and politics. Why? Even proficient readers must adapt their reading skills and strategies as new literacies emerge. Plus, libraries are bright spots in most schools, so showcasing them leaves visitors with a happy imprint.

KEY IDEAS

Each- and all-child legislation carry different messages—learn the difference.

The staff surrounding a legislator wields considerable power in how that legislator will vote.

Showcasing schools, staff, and children puts a face on educational issues.

Writing to legislators makes a difference.

EDUCATION ADVOCATE ACTION POINTS

Learn legislative language and be able to apply it to specific examples within your education context.

Take the time to build a relationship with staffers in your state and in Washington.

Invite delegates and congressional leaders into schools, and include each one's staff in the invitation.

Write letters to members to present your perspective on educational issues—and encourage other educators to do the same.

QUESTIONS FOR REFLECTION

What are my worst fears about getting involved at the state and federal levels? Why?

Who do I know who is already engaging in state and national conversations? What mentoring might they be willing to provide?

What legislative agendas are my education associations promoting?

What local stories related to national education issues can I share with legislators?

What do I know about my members' voting records and positions on education issues? How will I go about learning more?

What aspects of my school or school system would I most like to share with legislators? Why?

8

MOVING FORWARD

*B*ob *arrives at school early, wanting to ensure that everything is ready for the state superintendent's visit. Ever since his principal told him of this event, he has been excited. Not only will her visit give him an opportunity to showcase the outstanding work of students in the school system, but it will also give him an opportunity to speak with her about local stories related to issues at the state and national levels.*

Initially, Bob wanted to teach during her visit, but the principal explained that she wanted a teacher leader who was an advocate for education and children to show the state superintendent around the school. Bob has spent the last 2 weeks collecting stories from other teachers so that while visiting classrooms, Bob can share with the state superintendent relevant examples and factual information.

He is excited, too, to showcase the school's new wing, which includes updated science labs with state-of-the-art equipment. The greenhouse behind the science wing allows students to study plant life in depth, a project that they share with students in horticulture classes. Bob knows that science and math education is frequently scrutinized and that the state superintendent will want to see how taxpayer dollars are being spent in this area.

Visiting science classes will also give Bob an opportunity to highlight the sheltered instruction that English-language learners receive. It took several years, but the school finally had the majority of the faculty trained in the Sheltered Instruction Observation Protocol (SIOP) so that English-language learners could have access to the finest teachers at every grade and in every discipline.

Bob looks over the carefully assembled media kit in his hands. Although this visit isn't a media event, the kit contains important information about the school and the school system that will provide information beyond what he can share during the state superintendent's visit. And he knows that the school system's public communications coordinator distributed a press release, so he grabs a couple of extra kits just in case the media show up to cover the story. Bob is ready.

✿ ✿ ✿

Beverly straightens her scarf and waits with Bob in the main office. Although she has given official tour duties for the state superintendent's visit to Bob, as the school principal, Beverly wants to be available to welcome the state superintendent to the school. Initially, she wanted to conduct the tour herself, but she decided that a teacher leader might make a more lasting impression. Plus, Beverly has complete confidence in Bob. Not only is he an outstanding teacher, but over the last few years, he has become quite an advocate for education. Beverly knows that Bob is fluent with the issues and will showcase the school beautifully.

Of course, over the last 2 weeks, Beverly has been equally busy preparing for the event. She has contacted the school system's public communications coordinator to ensure that a press release was distributed to the media. She has fielded several phone calls, and she knows that the local news is planning to have a reporter cover the visit. Beverly has also requested updated copies of the school newsletter, the literary magazine, and fine arts events flyers and has ensured that they were added to the media kits.

And during her classroom walk-throughs earlier in the week, Beverly paid special attention to the hallway displays of student work and the bulletin boards for announcements, taking down any outdated flyers. The school looked good by any standard, but it looked especially good when considering that, aside from the new science wing, the building was 50 years old. The state superintendent's visit was quite a birthday present!

BRINGING OTHERS ALONG

According to Heath and Heath (2006), "once we know something . . . we find it hard to imagine not knowing it" (p. 1). You can't remember what it was like not being able to read, count, or even tie your shoes. You might recall the frustration of learning these tasks, but you can't ever remember what it was like not to know them.

Have you witnessed a child making the connection between speech and print and finally understanding what it means to read? Her face, awash with pride, lights up instantly. In that instant of understanding, in that moment of knowing, she forgets what it was like not to read. And from that moment, she will tell everyone she meets that she can read. More than that, she will read to her stuffed animals, "teaching" them what she has learned. What a celebration!

The same should be true for educators as they move from being leaders in the field to being advocates for education. We must celebrate what we have learned, the skills of advocacy, and we must nurture those skills in others.

Mentoring

Bringing others along can be a scary prospect, particularly if you are still finding your own way along the path to advocacy.

Mentoring, the most effective means to ensure personal connections to any new process, doesn't require that you know everything in advance, just that you are further along on the path.

The first time that I mentored a new teacher, I spent too much time worrying that the process would only allow others to confirm that I was completely incompetent. I thought that I needed to have all the answers, and I was positive that I didn't have them. It didn't help that I was younger than the teacher whom I mentored, and I worried that she wouldn't feel the need to listen to anything that I had to offer.

One day, she came to me, frustrated with a group of students who were struggling with a text that she was teaching. She knew that she knew the text. She knew that she could teach it. But she didn't know how to adapt her instruction to meet the needs of this particular group of learners. I gave her a few suggestions, none of which were foolproof because so much of instruction depends on too many factors to control for all of them. A week later, when we met in her room over lunch, she asked, "How did you know that would work?" I admitted that I didn't know. I admitted that I was banking on some similar experiences that I had had and the lessons that I learned from those experiences and that I was hoping that they would apply to and successfully remedy this situation. And it had. But if it hadn't, that wasn't a crisis. We would simply continue to try, to ask others for ideas, and to move forward.

In that moment, I learned that mentoring doesn't mean that you have all the answers; it means that you are willing to help another person find the answers. If my original suggestions hadn't worked, I would have suggested something else, confided in another colleague to get ideas—or something. I would have walked right alongside her in the search for the answers.

As a new education advocate, you don't have to have all the answers. No one does. What you need is a little more experience and the desire to bring someone else along. Just reading this book has given you additional experience. So, it's time to step up.

If you get a little lost, look to others who are ahead of you on the path. Check in with your education associations—you do belong to several now, right?—and ask their government relations staff or media relations staff to help guide you. These are people who advocate for education for a living, and they have the expertise and desire to help you.

Remember that more ideas are likely to produce the right idea. Work with others, not in isolation. Advocacy is hard enough; going it alone doesn't have any advantages. Mentoring others will only strengthen your own abilities and build confidence.

Tips for Mentoring

Touch base regularly. This doesn't have to be every week, but you should have some scheduled times to talk or meet face-to-face. Even if you discuss only your own children, you will be building a trust relationship and opening up networking opportunities.

Learn together. It's really all right not to have all of the answers. Tell your protégé that you are still navigating the waters of advocacy yourself.

Do your research. If you don't know the answer, fine, but don't disseminate false information. Use the resources available to you—education associations, staffers, other educators, business leaders, and so on—to find accurate information.

Network together. It's guaranteed that you and your protégé know different people. Use that to your advantage by hosting informal get-togethers to strengthen your networks.

Work with another mentor. Whether formally or informally, bouncing ideas off other mentors strengthens your own abilities. Many organizations have regular meetings during which advocates and advocacy mentors meet to discuss the issues, vent their frustrations with mentoring, and celebrate their successes.

ENGAGING IN THE CONVERSATION

As you work to bring others along, you must also strengthen your own advocacy skills. It's not enough to read this book, put it down, and do what you have always done. Children and education need a voice—in our communities, in our states, and in our nation. You must become part of that voice.

Get involved. Get involved at every level. One letter, one e-mail, one phone contact may not feel big, but combined with other letters, e-mail, and phone calls, educators can and do make a difference in their communities and in Washington.

Understand that starting on a new path often causes anxiety and a sense of insecurity. Here are some tips to help you get started and document your growth.

Sign up for electronic newsletters and updates available through education associations to which you belong. When those updates call for action, get involved.

Attend meetings in your community when education issues are discussed. Take time to really listen to what others are saying and to respond with factual information.

Go to school board meetings. Realistically, unless you are the superintendent or a member of the school board, you won't have time to attend every meeting, but make a point of attending several each year, especially when issues that will come before the school board are being covered in the media. Hearing public comment and school board member discussion firsthand is an important step to deeply understanding the issues facing your community and education as a whole.

Build a relationship with stakeholders in your community and with staffers in Washington. Keep a log with a separate page for each person, and record the dates, times, and gist of your conversations. Before each contact, review your notes from previous contacts.

Build a partnership around student learning and student achievement. If you haven't reached out to a local business for more than coupons, begin today to form a real partnership that will benefit kids.

Document your growth. Start a file to hold the various contacts that you make around advocacy efforts. Include business cards of people you meet, letters you have written to members of Congress, and articles on issues in which you have interest.

Know that advocacy is hard work and that large institutions such as schools and government generally move slowly. Regulations, budgets, appropriations, and other processes all take time. You won't see change overnight. You won't see change in a week. You probably won't see large change in a year. Stay with it. Remember that the experts at your education associations work with legislators in 2-year time frames, so afford yourself the time necessary to make effective change.

Finally, commend yourself for taking real steps to significant change. If all 3 million educators in the nation were to take the same step, we would become an enormous voice for education, learning, and children. Like a child learning to walk one step at a time, educators must become a strong voice for education one voice at a time.

KEY IDEAS

Once we know, we must share that knowledge with others.

Mentoring doesn't mean that you have all the answers; it means that you are willing to help another person find the answers.

Education advocacy benefits everyone.

EDUCATION ADVOCATE ACTION POINTS

Talk to someone about the importance of education advocacy—
a teacher, an administrator, a parent, a business partner,
anyone.

Connect a colleague to an education association that will provide
meaningful information and advocacy updates in that person's
area of expertise and interests.

Invite others to forums, meetings, and events that you will attend that advocate for education and the needs of children.

QUESTIONS FOR REFLECTION

Who will serve as my mentor?

Who will I mentor?

For which issue or issues do I have the most passion? Knowledge? Ability to affect? Why?

What is the step that I will take today to be a stronger voice for
education?

What is my advocacy goal for this month? For this academic
year? What evidence will I have to demonstrate achievement
of these goals?

FINAL THOUGHTS

My favorite ancient saying, the one that I keep on my desk, says,
"No one is a failure in this world who lightens a burden for someone else." Whether your advocacy efforts make small changes
that have a big impact in your school or community or whether

your advocacy efforts make big changes in legislation affecting every school in the nation, know that your efforts on behalf of education matter. By speaking out, you lighten the burden for those who walk with you and for those who follow. And together, those voices have significant impact—on schools, on the system, and, most important, on student learning.

AFTERWORD:
UPDATES AT PRESS TIME

Like any book, from writing to press to public takes time, and this text is no exception. And over time, situations change. This section provides updates on congressional issues as this book goes to press.

FISCAL YEAR 2007 BUDGET

Because education advocates made their voices heard on January 31, 2007, the House voted, and on February 14, 2007, the Senate voted to provide a $1.17 billion increase for education over Fiscal Year 2006 levels. The Senate designated most of these monies ($615.4 million) to raise the maximum Pell Grant to $4,310. Additionally, the following allocations were made: $250 million to support Title I of No Child Left Behind, $200 million supporting state grants under Individuals With Disabilities Education Act, and $104 million to support Head Start. The bill awaits the president's signature.

FISCAL YEAR 2008 BUDGET

Despite Congress' recent votes to increase funding for education, the president's proposed Fiscal Year 2008 budget calls for decreased funding for K–12 education. Although the proposed budget increases funding for Title I by $1.2 billion and funding for high school assessment development, it also eliminates 43 programs, including cutting in half state grants for career and technical education. Moreover, some increased funding, such as $250 million for Promise Scholarships, supports practices not proven to be educationally sound or effective.

HEAD START

The Senate Committee on Health, Education, Labor, and Pensions supports the Head Start for School Readiness Act. This bill calls for Head Start to align standards with early childhood learning standards and with local school systems. Additionally, eligibility criteria would be expanded to include a greater number of children.

APPENDIX A:
BIBLIOGRAPHY OF BUSINESS TITLES

Barr, L., & Barr, N. (1989). *The leadership equation.* Austin, TX: Eakin Press.

Bennis, W. G., & Biederman, P. W. (1997). *Organizing genius: The secrets of creative collaboration.* Cambridge, MA: Perseus Books.

Bennis, W. G., & Thomas, R. J. (2002). *Geeks and geezers: How era, values, and defining moments shape leaders.* Boston: Harvard Business School Press.

Blanchard, K., Carlos, J. P., & Randolph, A. (2001). *The 3 keys to empowerment.* San Francisco: Berrett-Koehler.

Collins, J. (2001). *Good to great: Why some companies make the leap . . . and others don't.* New York: HarperCollins.

Covey, S. R. (1989). *The 7 habits of highly effective people.* New York: Fireside.

Gladwell, M. (2000). *The tipping point: How little things can make a big difference.* New York: Little, Brown.

Gladwell, M. (2005). *Blink: The power of thinking without thinking.* New York: Little, Brown.

Goleman, D. (1995). *Emotional intelligence: Why it can matter more than IQ.* New York: Bantam Books.

Goleman, D. (1998). *Working with emotional intelligence*. New York: Bantam Books.

Goleman, D., Boyatzis, R., & McKee, A. (2002). *Primal leadership: Realizing the power of emotional intelligence*. Boston: Harvard Business School Press.

Greenleaf, R. K. (1977). *Servant leadership*. New York: Paulist Press.

Hybels, B. (2002). *Courageous leadership*. Grand Rapids, MI: Zondervan.

Johnson, S. (1998). *Who moved my cheese?* New York: G. P. Putnam.

Kotter, J. P. (1996). *Leading change*. Boston: Harvard Business School Press.

Lundin, S. C., Paul, H., & Christensen, J. (2000). *Fish!* New York: Hyperion.

Maxwell, J. C. (1998). *The 21 irrefutable laws of leadership*. Nashville, TN: Thomas Nelson Press.

Maxwell, J. C. (2006). *The difference maker*. Nashville, TN: Nelson Business.

McGinty, S. M. (2001). *Power talk: Using language to build authority and influence*. New York: Warner Books.

Michelli, J. A. (2007). *The Starbucks experience*. New York: McGraw-Hill.

Ortberg, J., & Walsh, S. (2001). *If you want to walk on water, you've got to get out of the boat*. Grand Rapids, MI: Zondervan.

Sherman, J. (1993). *Robert's rules of order*. New York: Barnes & Noble Press.

Snead, G. L., & Wycoff, J. (1997). *To do, doing, done!* New York: Fireside.

Spears, L. C., & Lawrence, M. (Ed.). (2002). *Focus on leadership: Servant-leadership for the 21st century*. New York: John Wiley.

APPENDIX B:
FEDERAL BUDGET CHARTS

Table AB.1. Federal Funding for Major Departments, 1998–2007 (in Millions of Dollars)

Department or Other Unit	1998	1999	2000	2001	2002	2003	2004	2005	2006	2007 estimate
Legislative Branch	2,593	2,612	2,892	3,036	3,204	3,411	3,905	4,007	4,128	4,306
The Judiciary	3,459	3,789	4,057	4,381	4,828	5,127	5,389	5,547	5,823	5,845
Agriculture	53,811	62,699	75,080	68,083	68,631	72,752	71,573	85,333	93,534	88,767
Commerce	4,037	5,021	7,789	5,004	5,313	5,666	5,830	6,149	6,373	6,179
Defense—Military	255,806	261,212	281,059	290,212	331,871	388,720	437,048	474,372	499,357	548,915
Education	31,294	31,285	33,477	35,523	46,373	57,145	62,780	72,858	93,429	68,040
Energy	14,414	15,879	14,971	16,319	17,669	19,379	19,893	21,271	19,649	21,988
Health and Human Services	350,358	359,455	382,340	425,922	465,373	504,957	542,994	581,456	614,315	671,254
Homeland Security	10,622	13,328	13,166	15,040	17,583	31,977	26,589	38,713	69,098	50,418
Housing and Urban Development	30,181	32,693	30,781	33,865	31,788	37,410	44,984	42,453	42,435	42,834
Interior	7,229	7,793	8,011	7,763	9,746	9,209	8,613	9,296	9,064	10,877
Justice	14,045	16,181	16,846	18,443	21,178	20,790	29,601	22,361	23,324	23,039
Labor	30,580	32,995	31,873	39,707	64,686	69,563	56,687	46,949	43,138	47,440
State	5,400	6,557	6,688	7,489	9,360	9,345	10,917	12,749	12,962	16,322
Transportation	35,554	37,672	41,555	49,231	56,252	50,764	54,879	56,596	60,139	63,775
Treasury	389,011	385,047	390,536	388,268	371,194	368,258	375,849	410,243	464,712	490,507
Veterans Affairs	41,752	43,155	47,075	45,044	50,902	56,950	59,583	69,844	69,807	72,325
Corps of Engineers	3,775	3,934	4,229	4,640	4,727	4,682	4,728	4,719	6,944	7,557
Other Defense—Civil Programs	31,216	32,014	32,864	34,164	35,157	39,883	41,730	43,483	44,436	47,636
Environmental Protection Agency	6,269	6,733	7,223	7,367	7,451	8,041	8,328	7,913	8,321	8,038
Executive Office of the President	237	417	283	246	451	386	3,349	7,686	5,379	2,677
General Services Administration	826	-413	74	-309	-684	589	-451	20	24	498
International Assistance Programs	8,937	10,071	12,089	11,810	13,292	13,457	13,657	15,039	13,944	17,061

NASA	14,194	13,636	13,428	14,095	14,405	14,610	15,152	15,602	15,125	16,143
National Science Foundation	3,188	3,283	3,487	3,690	4,188	4,732	5,116	5,434	5,542	5,860
Office of Personnel Management	46,297	47,519	48,655	50,894	52,540	54,135	56,547	59,500	62,400	58,802
Small Business Administration	−77	57	−421	−570	493	1,558	4,075	2,502	905	675
Social Security Administration (On-budget)	37,542	40,021	45,121	40,007	45,816	46,333	49,008	54,556	53,252	55,740
Social Security Administration (Off-budget)	370,069	379,213	396,169	421,257	442,011	461,401	481,200	506,779	532,491	567,179
Other Independent Agencies (On-budget)	10,884	6,193	8,809	11,392	16,713	14,582	10,109	16,779	14,008	16,066
Other Independent Agencies (Off-budget)	217	1,021	2,029	2,302	−651	−5,245	−4,130	−1,791	−1,075	2,642

Note: From the Office of Management and Budget (2006).

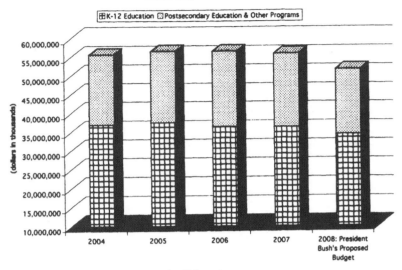

Figure AB.1. Federal Budget for Education

APPENDIX C:
SAMPLE LETTER TO CONGRESS

[letterhead]
[date]
Dear Congressman [surname]:

I am writing to urge you, as a member of the House of Representatives, to propose and vote for a budget that restores funding for education. On March 16, 2006, the Senate passed bipartisan amendments that would add $7 billion for education, health, and workforce training and add $2 billion for IDEA. These monies do not increase funding for education; they simply restore funding to the 2005 levels.

Although federal funds account for a small portion of any school division's overall budget, those funds are often allocated for our neediest students. Without them, staffing and programs are cut, and the very children who begin at a deficit remain behind their peers. In [school system], we have lost several Title I teachers over the last two years; this loss was due to federal budget cuts. Furthermore, some programs, such as Extended Day Enrichment, must be self-sustaining in our division, but it is programs such as this that meet the needs of students whose parents work and/or cannot afford other after school options.

The President's proposed budget will devastate entire educational programs, such as Perkins Career and Technical Education, Safe and Drug Free Schools, and Title II. Furthermore, cuts in Title I and IDEA impact classrooms beyond intervention and special needs. Additionally, the across-the-board cuts he recommends impact *every* child in the educational system.

When we lose funding, school divisions must make decisions to reduce monies for staffing, instructional materials, and programs. Just like every business, we have nonnegotiable expenses—busses, phones, heating, and the like. These expenses must be covered first, thus leaving the only "negotiables" in those areas that directly impact children and their learning. Yes, this is a complex problem. Rising energy costs cut into funds available for classroom materials, support staff, and programs.

Furthermore, funding cuts at the federal level impact every classroom. IDEA does not allow for provisions to reduce staffing or cut programs related to students with disabilities. Therefore, local dollars must be allocated to sustain these programs, thus reducing the monies available to support the regular curriculum. Additionally, NCLB requirements state that all students must achieve and demonstrate growth. But to meet the needs of *every* child, we must meet the needs of *each* child. To do this, we must have the support of federal, state, and local governments.

Public education is tasked with an enormous charge—one educators take on with great enthusiasm and verve. We are individuals who truly want to do right by children. We must have appropriate funding to meet our goals to prepare children to live and work in a global community.

At this critical juncture in the budget process, it is imperative that you and other members of the House take seriously your responsibility to *represent* your constituents. We must take seriously the education of our children. Please vote only for a budget that will, as a beginning, restore funding to 2005 levels. It is a necessary first step in assuring that all children will be able to succeed as citizens.

Sincerely,
Sandra Whitaker, NBCT
6–12 Language Arts Coordinator

APPENDIX D:
APPROPRIATE SALUTATIONS FOR
GOVERNMENT OFFICIALS

The left column under each title represents the appropriate address designation. The right column under each title represents the appropriate salutation.

PRESIDENT OF THE UNITED STATES

The President	Dear Sir (or Madam):
The President and Mrs. ____	Mr. President:
The President and Mr. ____	Madam President:
	Dear Mr. (or Madam) President:

VICE PRESIDENT OF THE UNITED STATES

The Vice President	Dear Sir (or Madam):
The Vice President and Mrs. ____	Mr. Vice President:
The Vice President and Mr. ____	Madam Vice President:
	Dear Mr. (or Madam) Vice President:

CHIEF JUSTICE

The Honorable (full name), Chief Justice of the United States

Dear Sir (or Madam):
Dear Mr. (or Madam) Chief Justice:

ASSOCIATE JUSTICE

The Honorable (full name)

Dear Sir (or Madam):
Dear Justice (surname):

CABINET OFFICER

The Honorable (name), Secretary of (office)

Dear Mr. (or Madam) Secretary:

SENATOR

The Honorable (full name)

Senator (full name)
Dear Senator:

REPRESENTATIVE

The Honorable (full name)

Representative (full name)
Dear Representative:

SPEAKER OF THE HOUSE

The Honorable Speaker   Dear Mr. (or Madam)
   of the House of Representatives   Speaker:

CHAIR OF A COMMITTEE

The Honorable (full name)   Dear Mr. Chairman:
                               Dear Madam Chairwoman:

GOVERNOR

The Honorable (full name),   Dear Sir or Madam:
   of (state)   Dear Governor (surname):

APPENDIX E:
GOVERNMENT WEBSITES

Agency	Website
Administration for Children and Families	www.acf.dhhs.gov
Administration on Developmental Disabilities	www.acf.hhs.gov/programs
Census Bureau	www.census.gov
Clerk of the House	www.clerk.house.gov
Congressional Information	www.congress.org
Congressional Record	www.gpoaccess.gov/crecord
Currently on the House Floor	www.clerk.house.gov/floorsummary/floor.php3
Democratic Congressional Campaign Committee	www.dccc.org
Democratic National Committee	www.democrats.org
Democratic Senatorial Campaign Committee	www.dscc.org
Department of Education	www.ed.gov
Department of Health and Human Services	www.dhhs.gov
Department of Homeland Security	www.dhs.gov
Federal Election Commission	www.fec.gov
Federal Register	www.archives.gov/federal_register
FirstGov	www.usa.gov
Government Printing Office	www.gpoaccess.gov
House Democratic Caucus	http://democrats.house.gov
House Republican Conference	www.gop.gov
Library of Congress	www.loc.gov
Library of Congress THOMAS	http://thomas.loc.gov

(continued)

Agency	Website
Office of Elementary and Secondary Education	www.ed.gov/about/offices/list/oese/index.html
Office of Head Start	www.acf.hhs.gov/programs/hsb/about/index.html
Office of Management and Budget	www.whitehouse.gov/omb
Office of Special Education and Rehabilitative Services	www.ed.gov/about/offices/list/osers/index.html
National Republican Congressional Committee	www.nrcc.org
National Republican Senatorial Committee	www.nrsc.org
Republican National Committee	www.rnc.org
Senate Democratic Conference	http://democrats.senate.gov
Senate Republican Conference	http://src.senate.gov
Supreme Court of the United States	www.supremecourtus.gov
United States House of Representatives	www.house.gov
United States Senate	www.senate.gov
United States Senate Calendar of Business	www.gpoaccess.gov/calendars.senate
The White House	www.whitehouse.gov

APPENDIX F:
EDUCATION ASSOCIATIONS
AND WEBSITES

Educators belong to thousands of various professional organizations based on interest and expertise. The goal of this page is to highlight a few of the national organizations representing different curricular and administrative responsibilities.

Education Association	Website
American Association for Gifted Children	www.aagc.org
American Association for the Mentally Retarded	www.aamr.org
American Association of School Administrators	www.aasa.org
American Educational Research Association	www.aera.org
American Educational Studies Association	www.aesa.org
American Federation of Teachers	www.aft.org
American Historical Association	www.historians.org
American School Counselor Association	www.schoolcounselor.org
Association for the Advancement of Computing in Education	www.aace.org
Association for Career and Technical Education	www.acteonline.org
Association for Health, Physical Education, Recreation, and Dance	www.aahperd.org
Association of Supervision and Curriculum Development	www.ascd.org
Council for Exceptional Children	www.cec.sped.org
Council of Chief State School Officers	www.ccsso.org
Education Commission of the States	www.ecs.org
International Reading Association	www.reading.org
International Society for Technology in Education	www.iste.org

(continued)

Education Association	Website
Music Teachers National Association	www.mtna.org
National Art Education Association	www.naea-reston.org
National Association for Bilingual Education	www.nabe.org
National Association for the Education of Young Children	www.naeyc.org
National Association of Elementary School Principals	www.naesp.org
National Association of Secondary School Principals	www.principals.org
National Board for Professional Teaching Standards	www.nbpts.org
National Council for the Social Studies	www.socialstudies.org
National Council of Teachers of English	www.ncte.org
National Council of Teachers of Mathematics	www.nctm.org
National Education Association	www.nea.org
National Middle School Association	www.nmsa.org
National Parent Teacher Association	www.pta.org
National School Boards Association	www.nsba.org
National Science Teachers Association	www.nsta.org
National Staff Development Council	www.nsdc.org
Society for Information Technology and Teacher Education	www.aace.org/site
Teachers of English to Speakers of Other Languages	www.tesol.org

BIBLIOGRAPHY

Ainsworth, L., & Viegut, D. (2006). *Common formative assessments: How to connect standards-based instruction and assessment.* Thousand Oaks, CA: Sage.

Albemarle County Public Schools. (2006). [Home page]. Retrieved August 1, 2006, from www.k12albemarle.org

American Association of School Administrators. (2006). [Home page]. Retrieved September 1, 2006, from www.aasa.org

Association for Supervision and Curriculum Development. (2006a). *ASCD advocacy guide.* Alexandria, VA: Author.

Association for Supervision and Curriculum Development. (2006b). [Home page]. Retrieved September 1, 2006, from www.ascd.org

Berry, B., Johnson, D., & Montgomery, D. (2005). The power of teacher leadership. *Educational Leadership, 62*(5), 56–60.

Bill and Melinda Gates Foundation. (2007). [Home page]. Retrieved November 1, 2006, from www.gatesfoundation.org

Boris-Schacter, S. (2006, March 15). Why aren't teachers weighing in on educational policymaking? *Education Week.* Retrieved March 24, 2006, from http://edweek.org/ew/articles/2006/03/15/27schacter.h25.html

Bransford, J. D., Brown, A. L., & Cocking, R. R. (Eds.). (2000). *How people learn: Brain, mind, experience, and school*. Washington, DC: National Research Council.

Burrup, P. E., Brimley, V., Jr., & Garfield, R. R. (1996). *Financing education in a climate of change* (6th ed.). Boston: Allyn & Bacon.

Castro, A. (2006, August 15). *Schools debate classroom spending rules*. Retrieved August 18, 2006, from http://dwb.newsobserver.com/24hour/nation/v-printer/story/3351072p-12336991c.html

Committee for Education Funding. (2006). [Home page]. Retrieved October 1, 2006, from www.cef.org

Congressional Management Foundation. (2005). *Communicating with Congress: How Capitol Hill is coping with the surge in citizen advocacy*. Washington, DC: Congressional Management Foundation.

Corporation for National and Community Service. (2007). *Learn and serve America*. Retrieved January 1, 2007, from www.learnandserve.org

Costa, A. L. (Ed.). (2001). *Developing minds: A resource book for teaching thinking* (3rd ed.). Alexandria, VA: Association for Supervision and Curriculum Development.

Cummins, J. (1984). *Bilingualism and special education: Issues in assessment and pedagogy*. San Diego, CA: College-Hill Press.

Cunningham, A., & Stanovich, K. (2003). Reading can make you smarter. *Principal*, 83(2), 34–39.

Darling-Hammond, L., & Bransford, J. (Eds.). (2005). *Preparing teachers for a changing world*. San Francisco: Jossey-Bass.

Department of Homeland Security. (2006). *Immigration*. Retrieved October 1, 2006, from www.dhs.gov/ximgtn

Dessoff, A. (2006, November). NCLB's purity. *District Administration*, pp. 43–46.

Dianis, L. (2006, November). By the numbers. *District Administration*, p. 90.

Dozier, T. (2006, March). *Influencing education in your classroom and beyond: An institute for teacher leadership*. Charlottesville, VA: State Farm National Board Certified Teachers Institute.

DuFour, R., & Eaker, R. (1998). *Professional learning communities at work*. Bloomington, IN: National Education Service.

Echevarria, J., Vogt, M., & Short, D. J. (2000). *Making content comprehensible for English language learners: The SIOP model.* Needham Heights, MA: Allyn & Bacon.

Gay, G. (2000). *Culturally responsive teaching: Theory, research, and practice.* New York: Teachers College Press.

George Lucas Educational Foundation. (2006). *Edutopia.* Retrieved October 1, 2006, from www.edutopia.org

Gershberg, A. I., & Hamilton, D. (2007, February 5). Bush's double standard on race in schools. *Christian Science Monitor.* Retrieved February 5, 2007, from www.csmonitor.com/2007/0205/p09s01-coop.htm

Global Source Education. (2007). *Media literacy in a post 9/11 world. Beyond September 11.* Retrieved January 1, 2007, from http://hrusa.org/september/activities/medialiteracy.htm

Glod, M. (2007, January 11). Fairfax vs. "No Child" standoff heats up. *Washington Post.* Retrieved January 24, 2007, from www.washingtonpost.com/wp-dyn/content/article/2007/01/10/AR2007011002542.htm

Hack, W. G., Candoli, I. C., & Ray, J. R. (1995). *School business administration: A planning approach* (5th ed.). Boston: Allyn & Bacon.

Heath, C., & Heath, D. (2006, December). The curse of knowledge. *Harvard Business Review, 84*(12), 20–23.

Hill, J. D., & Flynn, K. M. (2006). *Classroom instruction that works with English language learners.* Alexandria, VA: Association for Supervision and Curriculum Development.

Howe, N., & Strauss, W. (2000). *Millennials rising: The next great generation.* New York: Vintage Books.

International Reading Association. (2006). [Home page]. Retrieved September 1, 2006, from www.reading.org

Junior Achievement. (2007). [Home page]. Retrieved February 1, 2007, from www.ja.org/about/about_history.shtml

Kusler, M. (2006, March). *Women education leaders in Virginia* [Conference]. Charlottesville, VA.

Law, B., & Eches, M. (1990). *The more than just surviving handbook: ESL for every classroom teacher.* Winnipeg, Manitoba, Canada: Peguis.

Learning First Alliance. (2005). *A practical guide to promoting America's public schools.* Retrieved September 10, 2006, from www.learningfirst .org/publications.pubschools/

Levine, M. (2003). *A mind at a time.* New York: Simon & Schuster.

Marx, G. (2000). *Ten trends: Educating children for a profoundly different future.* Arlington, VA: Educational Research Service.

Marzano, R. J., Pickering, D. J., & Pollock, J. E. (2001). *Classroom instruction that works: Research-based strategies for increasing student achievement.* Alexandria, VA: Association for Supervision and Curriculum Development.

National Center for Education Statistics. (2006). [Home page]. Retrieved November 1, 2006, from http://nces.ed.gov/index.asp

National Council of Teachers of English. (2006). [Home page]. Retrieved September 1, 2006, from www.ncte.org

National Education Association. (2006). [Home page]. Retrieved September 1, 2006, from www.nea.org

National School Boards Association. (2006). [Home page]. Retrieved September 1, 2006, from www.nsba.org

National Service-Learning Clearinghouse. (2007). [Home page]. Retrieved January 1, 2007, from www.servicelearning.org

Nike. (2007). *Nikebiz.com.* Retrieved February 1, 2007, from www.nike .com/nikebiz/nikebiz.jhtml?page=0

Office of Elementary and Secondary Education. (2007). *President's FY 2008 education budget: Building on progress.* Retrieved February 20, 2007, from www.ed.gov/about/overview/budget/budget08/factsheet.html

Office of Head Start. (2006). *About Head Start.* Retrieved October 1, 2006, from www.acf.hhs.gov/programs/hsb/about/index.htm

Office of Management and Budget. (2006). *Budget of the United States Government Fiscal Year 2007.* Washington, DC: U.S. Government Printing Office.

Office of Management and Budget. (2007). *Budget of the United States Government Fiscal Year 2008.* Washington, DC: U.S. Government Printing Office.

Pascopella, A. (2006a, September). Inside the law. *District Administration,* p. 24.

Pascopella, A. (2006b, November). Does K–12 make sense? *District Administration,* pp. 56–61.

Rhodes, L. A., & Deming, W. E. (2004, October). *W. Edwards Deming Institute annual fall conference*. Washington, DC.

Schweinhart, L. J. (2005). *The High/Scope Educational Research Foundation Perry Preschool study through age 40*. Retrieved January 1, 2007, from www.highscope.org/research/perryproject/perryage40 _sumweb.pdf

Scott, K. (2006, September). *Leadership for effective advocacy and practice* [Institute]. Washington, DC: Association for Supervision and Curriculum Development.

Singleton, G. E., & Linton, C. (2005). *Courageous conversations about race: A field guide for achieving equity in schools*. Thousand Oaks, CA: Sage.

Stiggins, R., Arter, J. A., Chappius, J., & Chappius, S. (2004). *Classroom assessment for student learning: Doing it right: Using it well*. Portland, OR: Assessment Training Institute.

Sturgeon, J. (2006, September). Scared straight. *District Administration*, pp. 48–58.

Teachers of English to Speakers of Other Languages. (2007). [Home page]. Retrieved January 1, 2007, from www.tesol.org

Tomlinson, C. A. (2003). *Fulfilling the promise of the differentiated classroom: Strategies and tools for responsive teaching*. Alexandria, VA: Association for Supervision and Curriculum Development.

U.S. Department of Education. (2006a). [Home page]. Retrieved September 1, 2006, from www.ed.gov

U.S. Department of Education. (2006b). *Individuals With Disabilities Education Act*. Retrieved September 1, 2006, from www.ed.gov/about/ offices/list/osers/index.html

U.S. Department of Education. (2006c). *No Child Left Behind Act*. Retrieved September 1, 2006, from www.ed.gov/nclb/landing.jhtml?src=pb

U.S. House of Representatives. (2006). [Home page]. Retrieved September 1, 2006, from www.house.gov

U.S. Senate. (2006). [Home page]. Retrieved September 1, 2006, from www.senate.gov

USA Weekend. (2006). *Make a Difference Day*. Retrieved November 1, 2006, from www.makeadifferenceday.com

Wallis, C., & Steptoe, S. (2006, December 10). How to bring our schools out of the 20th century. *Time*. Retrieved January 24, 2007, from http://time.com/time/printout/0,8816,1568480,00.html

Washington Early Learning Fund. (2007). *Thrive by Five*. Retrieved January 1, 2007, from http://thrivebyfivewa.org

WestEd. (2007). [Home page]. Retrieved January 1, 2007, from www.wested.org

White House. (2006). [Home page]. Retrieved September 1, 2006, from www.whitehouse.gov

ABOUT THE AUTHOR

Sandra Whitaker is a National Board certified teacher in English language arts, and she serves as the secondary language arts curriculum coordinator for Albemarle County Public Schools. She has spent much of her career working with struggling readers and writers and is deeply concerned with issues of literacy, access, and differentiation. Integrating technology into high-quality English instruction and providing students with opportunities to reach across content areas are particular interests of hers. Additionally, she has written a 3-year leadership program using a concept-based design to address leadership skills and theory while connecting to core subjects.

Throughout her career, Whitaker has served the educational community as a teacher, building-level administrator, curriculum developer, and curriculum coordinator. She has presented sessions at annual conferences for the Association for Supervision and Curriculum Development, National Council of Teachers of English, International Reading Association, and National Board Certified Teachers, as well as consulted with schools implementing her leadership program and through the Association for Supervision and

Curriculum Development Faculty Program. She holds bachelor degrees in English and speech communications from Metropolitan State College of Denver and master of education and specialist in education degrees in educational leadership and administration and supervision from the State University of West Georgia. She is pursuing a doctorate in curriculum and instruction at the University of Virginia.

Made in the USA
San Bernardino, CA
19 May 2018